Images of Personal Value

Philip Mooney

Sheed & Ward

Sheed & Ward™ is a service of The National Catholic Reporter Publishing Company.

Library of Congress Cataloguing-in-Publication Data
Mooney, Philip, 1926-
    Images of personal value / Philip Mooney.
      p.   cm.
    Includes bibliographical references.
    ISBN: 1-55612-705-7
    1. Values. 2. Self-esteem. 3. Friendship. 4. Catholics in literature. I. Title.
BD435.M635 1994
128—dc20   94-19425
                                          CIP

Published by: Sheed & Ward
                   115 E. Armour Blvd.
                   P.O. Box 419492
                   Kansas City, MO 64141

To order, call: (800) 333-7373

For all those
eternally young persons
from "Butch" O'Hare to Charlie von Stade
who gave their last and best for us
fifty years ago . . .

Contents

- 1 -

Home

WHAT'S YOUR FAVORITE CHRISTMAS SONG? OR CAROL? FOR CAROL,
mine is "*Adeste Fideles*" sung by John McCormack on an old 78 record as we opened our presents beneath the tree. Dad, like so many
Irish-Americans of his generation, couldn't hear enough of the bard of
Athlone, who sang his words as clearly as if he were speaking. This
Christmas memory is dotted with oranges, for Dad insisted we each
eat a navel to make up for all the peppermint canes we had been
sword-swallowing. Mom took care of our birthdays—she would bake a
cake of our own choosing, mine being devil's food with sliced bananas
between the layers: delicious! But Christmas was Dad's time. He was
Pére Noël, though he never had to climb into a red velvet suit. His
grin was so authentic that we knew the Sears-Roebuck Santa was a
ho-hum imitation.

Bing Crosby was part of our Christmas too—singing some of the
songs in English we had just heard the choir sing at the Mass at dawn.
(No joke—the solemn celebration in our parish was at 5:00 in the
morning, and since my brother and I were in the choir we all made
haste like the shepherds to the church créche with half-awake mum-
bling.) Bing was a singer Mom and Dad could agree upon, since Mom
liked opera and Dad did not. I too liked his natural way of singing,
and his rendition of "*I'll Be Home for Christmas*" is still my favorite
Christmas song. It has special meaning for me. I had gone far away
to college and didn't get home for Christmas again until after Dad had
died. I share this biographical note with you to point up the meaning
of home. Antoine de Saint Exupéry speaks of home as "the essential
that remains from what one has experienced in customs and family

1

feasts—the house of memories."[1] He would agree that home is where we grew up, where we get our mail from, where we store our images of childhood. He remarks that "the essential is to live for the return,"[2] and we Americans agree with the French aviator: home is where we go at Christmas.

Why do we Americans, believers and unbelievers alike, crowd our highways and airports to be home for Christmas? I'm quite sure most people would make the question their answer: "Well, of course, just to be home!" Fair enough! But then, what is the meaning of home for you, for me? You must believe in home or you wouldn't turn yourself into an Alsatian pretzel schedule-wise and luggage-wise to find your way there at Christmas time. One thing is sure: Home is not where you hang your hat—you left it in the taxi in your rush to get *home*.

Home is not merely an address—that's where your house is and the house most often stands for home, but, as Saint Exupéry insisted before World War II took him, "Men die for a home—not walls or furniture."[3] Home is made up of those special persons who occupy a corner of our heart. In fact, if you ask yourself whom you would most like to spend Christmas with, you have pretty well described home for yourself. Tennessee Williams was so accurate in saying that home is not "a place, a building, a house of wood, bricks, stone. I think of a home as being a thing that two people have between them in which each can nest, rest—live in, emotionally speaking."[4]

Curious thing that Tennessee Williams would find home in the relationship between just two people, especially when we think of Christmas as a household bulging with children, relatives and friends. In fact, our hearts abound with those special friends we would like to be with on Christmas day but cannot. (Anne Lindbergh is onto something when she says the human heart is infinite—and AT&T does help because the voice of a far-off friend that day becomes a personal Christmas bell.) Yet, when you come right down to it, Tennessee Williams is quite perceptive: The particular bond of friendship that a daughter has with her father is not the same as the one she has knit with her husband or her son or her old girlfriend from college. Each bond of friendship is individual and never duplicated, precisely because it is a relationship between two unique persons. You will know this when someone very close to you dies—what you miss about your friend is simply and profoundly his or her unique spirit that is irreplaceable. Someone else may come along and claim your time and interest, but no one will ever take the place of your beloved, nor will your relationship with anyone else ever make up for the bond you shared with her.

Parents learn this quite early on. For though their communication with each other over long years of courtship and marriage has reached such an interior sensitivity that even a pause speaks a paragraph, they cannot hope that each child of theirs will become equally close to both of them. They respect the individual personality of each of their children and would agree that home is a network of all those unique ties we form with each of those special persons who mean most.

But perhaps home is best described as "Your welcoming shoulder." This is where it has ever been since we first experienced belonging. After our difficult entry into this chilly world of blinding light, our mother gently brought her baby to her bosom with our head nestling naturally upon her shoulder. The returning soldier or sailor finds it there as his 10-year-old daughter breaks from the group on the tarmac, runs and leaps into the arms of Dad, gives him a kiss, and rests her head upon his shoulder. It is where hellos and good-bys are whispered. There are, of course, all different ways of expressing love in family and friendship. But our sense of belonging always comes to rest upon Your welcoming shoulder.

This welcome presumes mutual love and affection. It cannot be a wooden gesture. There can be no shying away, or the spontaneous openness of friendship just isn't there. Many of us are squeamish about showing affection, but the welcome must be sincere even if the embrace is momentary. Without this mutual sincerity, we are not truly in touch and we'll have to play the role of friends without really being friends. But then we are not being ourselves and are not really at home. This charade can be draining, as Anne Lindbergh says so well. Comparing home to a channeled whelk in her refreshing book, *Gift from the Sea,* Mrs. Lindbergh says that she will only let true friends into her shell because she finds insincerity so exhausting. Her author-friend and fellow air-pioneer, Antoine de Saint Exupéry, could not agree with her more. In his beautiful little tribute to friendship, *Lettre à un otage,* St-Ex describes the sterling sincerity of a welcoming friend wherein a person experiences home: "I need to go where I am completely myself . . . I know you are willing to take me just as I am. What do I have to do with a friend who judges me?"[5]

St. Exupéry says it all: Home is where I can be completely myself all the time without being put under scrutiny. There is no fear of being rejected if I should say the wrong thing or if in not feeling up to par I step on your toes. Consequently, the primordial image of personal value that home instills is that *I am acceptable just as I am* with the qualities and characteristics that are mine alone. That's why we love Christmas so much. Nobody asks me whether I got a raise at work or makes my high-school daughter squirm by asking her about her PSAT scores. These questions are of no significance in the ambience of the manger at Bethlehem where only poor shepherds came.

At home, I don't have to measure up to some preconceived notion of what I am supposed to be in the mind of a supposed friend. For, as St-Ex intimates, there is an unconditional dimension that marks true friendship. This means that my closest friend is free to be herself, too. So, I don't expect her to tie herself into a knot trying to anticipate my every need and to steer clear of my particular sensitivities. The depth of our relationship does not ebb and flow with our friend's every blue mood. In friendship we accept the friend just as he or she is.

There is, however, another dimension to friendship that is conditional: This becomes painfully evident when a friend who was once affectionate, thoughtful, and appreciative turns cold and uncommunicative and critical of most of my decisions and preferences. No friend can put up with this turnabout for very long because the one condition of friendship is to be a friend. And to be a friend is to act as friend. This life is not a trial run. So, though my love for my friend may remain out of deep appreciation for her basic goodness and fond memories of our happy times together, the mutuality essential to friendship is shaky. This breakdown in communication between friends may turn upon the fear of intimacy that psychologists claim has been symptomatic of the 80s.[7] But no true friend falls into a pattern of keeping the other at a distance.

We are getting a bit far from "home," even in pointing up by contrast why we feel so unconstrained in the presence of a true friend. But what is the positive meaning of "being completely yourself"?

Only you can respond to that question in the concrete circumstances of your life, but two things are certain: No institution can impose it and there is risk involved for you to discover your full self. When Brendan Behan was leaving the security of the "borstal" or workhouse for boys that had become so familiar to him, an officer said to him, "It must be wonderful to be free." Brendan's response was a wistful "It must."[8] Spoken as the curtain-line of the Irish author's autobiographical play, *Borstal Boy*, these two words carry all the nuances of an uncertain future and necessary challenge that finding one's true self implies. This need for risk to become a complete person is wonderfully stated in a citation a student wrote out for me on a Thank You card the last day of one of my courses:

Risk

To laugh
is to risk seeming a fool=
To weep
is to risk seeming sentimental=
To reach out for another
is to risk involvement=
To express feelings
is to risk revealing your true self=
To share your vision with a group
is to risk ridicule=
To love
is to risk not being loved in return=
To sacrifice for another
is to risk dying=
To hope
is to risk disappointment=
To try at all
is to risk failure=
But, risk we must!
For the greatest hazard in life
is to risk nothing:
The person who risks nothing
becomes nothing
and belongs to no one!

This poem sets the totally open context within which we are searching—to find ourselves in key images of personal value and in keen awareness of the perspectives that determine our foresight, insight and even our hindsight. This means that we must now take a good look at the various institutions that influence our living and can get in the way of our finding home on Your welcoming shoulder.

- 2 -

Institutions

NEAR THE END OF HER LONG LIFE, MY MOTHER SHARED HER PHOTO album with me. We came across a photo she had taken on my first day at school: I was done up in shorts, kneesocks, white shirt and tie—very *de rigueur* for the times—but quite grim-faced. On the back of the photo my mother had written: "Look what the first day of school has done to a happy-go-lucky boy." It was my first day away from home: I had entered the world of institutions.

In our infancy, we experienced the sense of being totally acceptable through the nearly constant attention and affection of our parents when we could do practically nothing for ourselves. Then came the years of tasks to be accomplished, from learning how to use a spoon to wiping the dishes. Early frustrations surfaced at not being quite able to accomplish what Mom and Dad were seeking from us. But, we could take the letdown and the swat on the rear when we were naughty because we trusted the affection our parents had for us. This was especially true if we were blessed with parents who did not make the age-old mistake of conditioning their love upon the performance of some assigned task—the "if you make a mess of your meal, Mommy won't love you" sort of thing. Our parents did shoosh us when we went to church with them, in perhaps our first confining experience of "institution." But no fear, since we were right next to Mom and Dad.

The first real rupture from home came on that first day of school. It was probably our first full-fledged experience of institution—when some lady we never saw before barked: "Get to your seat." I remember having to keep your head down on the desk cradled in your arm, ready to start the day with The Lord's Prayer. If your head popped up before Amen, you got a crack on the knuckles with the teacher's not-so-Golden ruler. I had learned my initial lesson about institutions: they have a way of making you squirm and feel guilty if you don't toe the line. In fact, this is where I absorbed the image of personal value that institutions impose: *I am acceptable only if I conform and perform according to the established norm.*

This happened in a public school in a small town in western Pennsylvania. Times have changed, but not long ago on a city bus in Strasbourg, France, the heavy side of institution made itself felt. A group of fifth-grade children headed for a class outing bunched onto the bus. A boy and girl rushed for the one empty seat at the head of the bus and squiggled in together. But the teacher singled out the little girl for punishment. Why, I hadn't a clue. The youngster was made to feel guilty by having to stand alone in the alcove of the bus—isolated from the rest. What bothered me deeply about this strange display of discipline was that the teacher had embarrassed the child in public outside of the classroom. What right did the elder Alsatian gentry and myself have to witness the "put-down" of this child who was merely scrambling for a seat? Institution had placed this little one under public judgment and she had done nothing wrong. She was made to feel unworthy of the company of her classmates on a trip they had looked forward to. Such scenes sear the soul—which is why our schools play such a sensitive role in our upbringing. At school the child is no longer home and has entered the larger world of institution where he or she will spend most waking hours for years to come. I have always felt that boarding schools are a limited blessing because there was no chance to be home even at the end of the day. The shadow of institution, however benign, is constantly there.

We have our private institutions like IBM, Exxon, the phone company, the Girl Scouts of America, and the AFL-CIO. Then there are the White House and Capitol dome in Washington, D.C. standing for our most prominent public institution: the government. Town hall on a small village green symbolizes the same—all those public institutions, like the water department and the city clerk's office responsible for the public welfare. I remember when all five of us children came down with the chicken pox in that same small Pennsylvania town: we were quarantined for all to know because the health officer had posted a scarlet sign on a tree in our front yard. I don't remember the fine

print but the headlines said in effect: "Stay away from this family—
they have the polka-dot plague with a capital P that stands for Pox."
Public institution was doing its duty.

Institutions do not deliver our identity but we cannot dispense
with them. They form the very structures of society. We cannot go
very far as individual persons unless we can count on the power company's supplying electricity for street lights, traffic lights, refrigerators
and, God save us, our computers. This is not to slight the gas company, the oil producers, the banks, and the police and fire departments.
We also need institutions like the churches and synagogues to reassure
us that there is a world even beyond government and utilities and that
the hidden center of this personal universe is a loving God.

As for our educational institutions, the best endorsement for
them comes from the children themselves. After a long vacation, they
are anxious to get back to school, much as they moan about homework. It is not just the instruction in the 3 R's and advancement in
higher learning that make schools so necessary to our personal growth.
Our schools train us how to get along with others and to work together
to accomplish long-term projects. We do have to learn how to take
our place in society and we do have to prepare ourselves to perform
well as good, reliable workers for our company. This involves putting
individual preferences aside in order to get the job done for our organization. Service for others and the need to earn a living are simply
part of being a mature person. We cannot each have our own way and
hope to get anywhere with others. This is true even in family and
friendship. But it is a *sine qua non* for social institutions and organizations, as John Macmurray emphasizes: "The satisfactory working of
social life depends upon entering into relationships with other people,
not with the whole of ourselves but only with part of ourselves."[1]

Macmurray sets in relief the central reason why we cannot fully
identify with any institution or organization. No institution engages
our complete self. Institutions serve a purpose which draws us to
them, even if it is a Vic Tanny gym where we work out to lose weight.
We also make our semi-weekly trips to mighty Exxon's local station
for another purpose: to keep our car running.

Maybe I need gas because what I look forward to all week is a
Saturday on the courts since I am much more talented at swinging a
tennis racket than slinging sacks at my post-office job. But even the

institution of sport, so dominant in the U.S.A., doesn't draw forth my full potential as a person, no matter how many tournaments I have won or how much time I have devoted to them. But wait, could not my identity be just that—carrying out a whole series of tasks, projects, or goals that engage my time and talent? This is a deserving question, but it prompts another: What becomes of our identity as a person if we lose our athletic or artistic talent in a car crash or if we face mandatory retirement and can no longer spend time on the job? The upshot is this: we cannot completely identify with institutions simply because they do not engage our full self in personal freedom.

We accept this limitation from government to a degree and from the company we work for to a degree. Constitutions specify this limit for government and contracts for business or industrial institutions. But what about our schools, our churches? They have heavily influenced the way we envisage the world and crimped our freedom to search out our own happiness in this world. How do we determine the appropriate level to which schools and churches may go in checking our freedom? And what about those neighborhood or society customs that have become unwritten standards—as rigid as those of any visible institution—that no one may violate without becoming an outcast? Neighborhood norms are an accurate reflection of a particular culture as shaped by its chief educational and ecclesiastical institutions. These twin forces have molded our attitudes towards marriage, family, morality, and images of acceptability.

Recall that Ronald Reagan was the first divorced person to be elected president when, 30 years earlier, Adlai Stevenson's divorce had hampered his candidacy. Recall that John F. Kennedy was the first Catholic to be elected president when, 32 years earlier, Governor Alfred E. Smith's Catholicism had broken the solid Democratic South and cost him the presidency. (His was a class act: when it became obvious that his election was lost, he turned to his aides in the New York hotel and said, "Thank you for all your work, but it is my wife Kate's birthday; so let's go upstairs and cut the cake.") And just a few years ago there was such shame attached to a girl's having a baby out of wedlock—the term itself has a jailhouse sound—that a clandestine abortion was often her only option if she were still to be accepted by family and friends. Vincent de Paul had to fight this prejudice three centuries earlier in Catholic France where he and Louise de Marillac started the first foundling home for the children of these mothers. But, how could such taboos prevail in the 20th century? Because of custom—that's all we can say while asking, who established custom? In the United States, Christianity with a distinctly puritan stripe going back to colonial times has fostered most of our customs. We must therefore take a careful look at the way the Church as institution has influenced the way we look at ourselves and others. By Church we mean mainstream Christian denominations, including the Roman Catholic Church in counter stance to which the Protestant Churches took their very name.

The Christian Church, whose institutional mission is to bring Jesus' "salvation" to the whole world, operates on a double premise: that its authority comes from Jesus as the revelation of God and that to disobey its teaching in faith and morals is to risk hell. The Church's chief claim to this prerogative is found in the final lines of Matthew's Gospel:

> All authority in heaven and on earth has been given to me: Go, therefore and teach all nations, baptizing them in the name of the Father and of the Son and of the Holy Spirit, teaching them to observe all I have commanded you; and, lo, I am with you all days even to the consummation of the world. (Mt. 28:18)

The sanction of eternal punishment for rejecting the apostolic teaching is stated at the end of Mark's Gospel: "He who believes and is baptized will be saved; but he who does not will be condemned." (Mk. 16:16) It should be added that down through the centuries, when the Roman Church held sole religious hegemony in western Europe, two other passages in Matthew were invoked to validate the authority of the pope and the bishops "to bind on earth as in heaven."

Two observations must be made immediately. First, Jesus formed a group to go proclaim his Good News, but he did not ask them to write a set of books. Consequently, there were Christian communities long before a single word of the New Testament had been put down in writing. As for the passages above, Scripture scholars today would insist that the Matthew statement may well not have been that of Jesus but a later insertion to endorse the apostolic authority that was then being transferred to the bishops. Matthew's Gospel was written a good 50 years after the death of Jesus, and when the Lord did not come again as soon as the Apostles had expected, they and their successors had to set up "church" to keep Jesus' teaching and their authority till the end of time. Valid as this authority may be, it cannot be based entirely upon the quotation from Matthew. So, to borrow a phrase from Lutheran theologian Karl Barth, we should be wary of turning these particular citations into "a paper Pope."

The other observation is that Jesus had only one commandment: "Love one another as I have loved you" (John 15:12). He instilled this norm at his Last Supper with his friends, where he also emphasized that he was "the way and the truth and the life." The truth that was to set us free was his very life—especially his crucifixion on Calvary, relieving us of the guilt of sin coupled with his Easter reunion with his own, dispelling the fear of death. Yet the institutional church managed to turn things around so that Christians were not free to search out all the truths of God's marvelous creation without stricture. If anyone did not adhere to the ecclesiastical injunctions, he or she was isolated from the community through excommunication or even put to death as a heretic. One of the slippages of history is that in the age when the beautiful French Gothic cathedrals like Chartres and Rheims were being completed, a 20-year-old girl was burnt at the stake. Her crime: she had refused to cave in to the Inquisition and forego her conviction that interior voices had inspired her to lead the armies of France against the invader and crown the Dauphin, yes, at Rheims. With the Bishop of Beauvais signing the decree of execution, this raw exercise of ecclesiastical power was a travesty of Jesus' commandment of love. Joan of Arc was crushed by the religious institution of her time, just as Jesus had been. His name was on her lips when the flames engulfed her.

We might think that such overwhelming enactment of church authority was an historical aberration. No, we have had thought control on the part of the Church right down to our own time. Roman Catholics were not permitted until recently to read the King James version of the Bible because of an edict from the Holy Office—that former Vatican bureau that was charged to maintain orthodoxy in faith and morals and provide all authoritative interpretations of the Scriptures. Galileo was not alone in coming up against this indomitable arbiter of Holy Writ. It was not until 1942—repeat: just 50 years ago—that Scripture scholars were given a free hand to consult the original Greek texts and employ all the scholarly tools of exegesis, hermeneutics, literary form and redaction criticism to search out the truthful meaning of the New Testament. Catch the drift here: Over the centuries, the Church would point to the cited passages from Matthew and Mark cited above to validate its prerogative to set up a Holy Office which, in turn, disallowed open scholarly research into those very texts. Pope Pius XII, a scholar himself, and his successors, John XXIII and Paul VI, changed all that and, in effect, affirmed that nothing in all of creation can threaten truth because this world is God's world and his Incarnational reality can be found within it if we but sharpen our powers of interior vision.

There's a plaque in Yankee Stadium, alongside those of Babe Ruth and Lou Gehrig, bearing the name of a former Cardinal, John Montini. He never played baseball but he brought a huge crowd to the Bronx stadium when he offered Mass there as Pope Paul VI—he had found God's presence when he visited the Jordan River where Jesus was baptized; he had found God's presence in kissing the shoe of Patriarch Athenagoras in Constantinople, thus healing a rift with the Greek Orthodox Church that had lasted a thousand years. He had found God's presence "in the house that" a non-Biblical "Ruth built." Pius XII had unlocked the doors of the Vatican, John XXIII had invited the whole world in for the Second Vatican Council, and Paul VI went out himself to take a good look at God's world in his well-considered visits. But this changeabout came two generations too late for playwright Eugene O'Neill.

O'Neill lived in the age of the Index of Forbidden Books. The Roman Church was so fearful in those days that certain books would harm the faith and morals of its members that it put out a long list of works Catholics could not read—*read*—under pain of sin. The roster is a Who's Who of prominent 18th and 19th-century thinkers: Kant, Hegel, Kierkegaard, Marx, Voltaire, Dumas. This last, Alexander Dumas, had written the *Count of Monte Cristo* and *The Three Musketeers*, but made the Index—maybe even the Top Ten—for anticlerical statements in some of his works. How thin-skinned the Church of fishermen had become.

Eugene O'Neill was a sixth-grader in a Catholic boarding school near Manhattan and was preparing for his first Communion. His father had come to town as star in the stage version of *The Count of Monte Cristo* and invited young Gene and a classmate down for a Saturday matinee. When the nun in charge of the class found out that the two boys had seen a play by an author on the Index, she scolded them and would not let them make their first Communion. What a miscarriage of school and church practice: to embarrass a child and exclude him from receiving the Sacrament that means most to Catholic children, simply because the boy had seen a play starring his Dad. Scars like this keep, so it is little wonder that by his late teens Eugene O'Neill had left his church altogether. (One of his last plays, *Days without End,* however, does probe the positive meaning of Jesus' crucifixion and resurrection in confronting the problems of guilt and death.) In this unhappy episode, the institutional side of Christianity had reneged on the kindness Christ mandated for his followers and implanted the very guilt this same Jesus had died to redeem. This stumbling block of institutional Christianity gives cause for pause.

I once had a young friend who knew exactly how to get me to back off when I became too insistent upon a line of action. (Well-meant advice can still be out of bounds because it hems in the spontaneity of personal choice. Better never to volunteer counsel than intrude upon a friend's full freedom to seek and find her own way in life. The probing may be the choicest part of the search for personal realization.) She would say, "You're making me feel guilty." This person, by her own frequent admission, was no saint. But she was, to put it neatly, a star. (Please allow me my liking for *neat* and its star-like connotations: It comes from the French word *nette* that means clear and clean or the German word *nette* that means kind and nice. With a nod to my Alsatian forebears, I favor both interpretations.) Each one of us is a star because Christ was born under one. This is not pious talk. We each take our lasting worth from sharing the humanity of this Jesus who was born as one of us. This is the significance of the Star of Bethlehem that led the wise men from the East to the presence of this child. This is the final truth about ourselves that sets us free: Each of us is "the prize"—priceless in the sight of the Father. This is the meaning of Christmas and the motive Jesus gives for being compassionate to others. As his parable of the Prodigal Son dramatizes, each person is the beloved of the Father. This is why it is such a violation of kindness to set ourselves up in judgment and make another, especially a friend or family member, feel guilty. This is the surest way to undermine a person's freedom to be himself or herself. It's a punch in the stomach, knocking out the spontaneity one seeks in friendship. My young acquaintance had been right—getting others to conform to what we want by insinuating a sense of guilt if they don't has no place in family or friendship. Jesus could not stand that "righteous" attitude of the Pharisees that was so quick to put down others as "sinners." And he was proud to call a former prostitute one of his best friends. (In John's Gospel account, Mary Magdalene was first to see Jesus on Easter day.) Yet, the institutional side of his Church has a way of making a person feel not quite worthy of God's love unless he or she conforms to "accepted practice."

My own Mom and Dad had to settle for the rectory office in Cairo, Illinois to celebrate their marriage. Dad was a Boston Irish Catholic and Mom was Methodist. Roman church practice in those days required Catholics to marry before a priest but would not let them make their vows to their Protestant bride or groom before the altar. The irony was that Mom was the organist in her church but had no music for her wedding. Years later this condescending attitude slowly began to thaw: first, the Protestant could get married in front of the altar rail in the Catholic church; then he or she was allowed into the sanctuary; and finally, the Protestant could marry the Catholic in his or her own church with the blessing of the Catholic bishop. We are talking about baptized Christians all around. The rectory marriage was my Dad's only option. The Catholic church would have considered him unmarried and living in sin if he had married Mom in her own church. I never heard my Mom or Dad complain about the rules governing their marriage. Mom even made the decision to share my Dad's faith-vision after the death of their first-born, Patricia. I register this family incident only as an example of how institutional practice could make a couple feel less than worthy if they didn't go along with the conditions set down for their most personal of days. Here again we have the image of personal value that institution imposes: I am acceptable only if I conform or perform according to the established norms of the institution.

How did the Church come to have such a grip on personal practice? Through pressure, the oldest pressure known to humankind—fear of exclusion from the company of friends, family and those who mean most. From the Biblical Cain to Shakespeare's Richard II, exile was the most dreaded of punishments. The institutional church put forward the double threat of excommunication from the Christian community on earth and banishment hereafter from the company of God and the blessed through condemnation to the exterior darkness of hell forever. This latter sanction was fairly formidable for the better part of the 20 centuries since Christ because the average life span had been so short. Nothing like the black plague to have a person ponder eternal verities.

We detect this threat of exclusion from community even in Matthew's Gospel where if a brother doesn't shape up, he is to be given the boot (Mt. 18:15-17). Remember that the key editorial concern of the Matthew account was to validate church! But excommunication still seems a far cry from Jesus' high regard for the blind man in John's Gospel. This man was banished from his synagogue for staying loyal to the Christ who had cured him. For this reason Jesus sought him out to acknowledge his fidelity. Personally, it is hard for me to justify excommunication—ever, in the light of this touching incident and Jesus' parable of the Prodigal Son whose Father never excluded him from the family home. It was the elder brother who wanted to keep him out, even as his fellow townspeople of Nazareth did Jesus. To be branded a public sinner through excommunication closes off the ease of repentance the adulteress experienced in Jesus' gentle treatment vis-à-vis the condemning Pharisees in the temple courtyard. (This suggests the chief reason my students give for avoiding church— the judgmental gossip of the communicants in the parking lot afterwards!) Jesus himself faced this same circle of institutional judgment on Good Friday morning. Later that dismal day, he confronted the Roman Empire in the person of Pontius Pilate and, insisting that his kingdom was not of this world, he explicitly rejected institutional power even as a way of saving himself from death.

Yet, after two and a half centuries of bloody persecution from the Caesars, Christianity through Constantine became the established religion of the Roman Empire. As the Church of Rome, it took on the structures and exercise of imperial power that in time became so engrained as to condemn a Joan of Arc to death. We can be brief here but not simplistic—the Christian Church, like every institution, has to maintain its identity and purpose through a set of principles. So, understandably, it requires its members to conform to these norms. But, Christianity has only one principle, the principle of Christ's kind of love. So, while its political counterpart, the Holy Roman Empire, reduces conformity to unswerving policy and conduct, Christianity can hardly do so and remain true to its foundational principle of compassion that respects the integrity of each person as son or daughter of the Father. Nothing could be further from Jesus' love that sets each person free to be himself or herself in full spontaneity than to insist upon uniformity of practice from each member of the community. But this the Church did with such stoic insistence that institutional obedience to established law eclipsed charity as the key Christian virtue.

Such was the neo-Pharisaism and crypto-Pelagianism that implied that we could earn heaven and God's friendship only through strict observance of Church and canon law. (Please excuse the Greek suffixes above: college professors love to use them because they sound so *avant garde,* when actually they are as old as the Sabine Hills. We professors can become fossils by immersing ourselves in antiquity!) Even down into our own time, Roman Church law dictated that if you did not observe the Friday abstinence from meat, you had committed a mortal sin which would send you to hell forever. Now, this was heresy because it was a practical denial of two central Christian truths: the Incarnation and Redemption. If you really believe that the Divine Son became human and was born as Jesus and that he died on the cross to save us from the consequences of our sin, how could he ever condemn us to hell for eating an Oscar Mayer hot dog? This precept is so ancient as regards Lenten abstention from meat that the three days before Ash Wednesday are called *Carneval*—"Goodbye, meat!" Since the prohibition itself made little sense—especially in light of the age-old exemption enjoyed by southern Spain for having routed the infidel Moors—its only validation was as something God required in obedience to the Church as his divine authority on earth. In my youth, I had let the proscription against meat on Friday overwhelm my practical faith and hope in the great truths that the divine Son loved me, even me—to borrow from St. Paul—and gave himself for me. Obedience to Church law in institutional Christianity had effectively obscured the grand truth of God's personal love for me as revealed in Jesus.

No one speaks more glowingly of God's love for us than Augustine of Hippo. But this Father of the Church had fathered a child in his youthful days when he was an avowed Manichaean. The Manichaeans were a sect that considered that the body and all its emotional, sexual and passionate expressions come from the creator-spirit of evil, whereas the soul, mind and spirit spring from the creator-spirit of good. This is pagan doctrine contradicting Genesis that dramatizes the goodness of all of God's creation and the Epistle to the Ephesians that includes the sexual union in marriage as symbolic of Christ's love for the Church. Augustine did have the good sense to name his child Deodatus (Gift of God), but he abandoned both the child and its mother for Italy, where he reclaimed his Christianity under Ambrose. His love for God stemmed from his "conversion" in which he experienced God's forgiveness of his wayward past.

Unfortunately for Christianity, the traces of Augustine's Manichaean bias cut so deep that his attitude towards marriage and sexuality was severely tainted. For Augustine sexual expression, even within marriage, is sinful unless it is justified by the spiritual intent to have children for God's kingdom. Abstinence from sexual expression in his Manichaean mind was a virtue, as was the prudence that could not be swayed by emotional considerations. (Augustine is not totally to blame for the disparaging attitude towards sexuality and marriage that infiltrated Christianity through his pen. The neo-Platonic culture of the times, in tandem with the Stoic policy of imperial Rome, had created a context that was ripe for the puritanism that would infect Christianity down to our own day. Cromwell's England may have invented the term but the puritan trend goes back to 5th-century times.) As passionate as Augustine could be in speaking of God's love for us, he turned ascetic when it came to our human love for one another. The spontaneity of affection for another person had to be kept within proper reserve (effusive show of affection is still acceptable only in the "moon-struck"), and sexual spontaneity even in marriage was restricted to the purpose of propagation. The spouses' sexual expression in mutual enjoyment of their personal union was *verboten*—to the denial of Ephesians and the dismay of married couples for centuries. This institutional stricture invading conjugal intimacy held firm in the medieval courtly romances until Gottfried von Strassburg's *Tristan* restored some balance to the Christian attitude towards human sexuality.

If obedience was the virtue that insured uniformity in Church discipline, chastity was the virtue that curbed the spontaneity in the expression of love for a friend or neighbor. Just as obedience displaced love as the sign of a follower of Christ in John's Gospel, chastity eclipsed marital love as the sign of Christ's love for the Church in Ephesians. The Church as institution could not engage our full potential as persons because obedience to its laws had cut back our options to live by the great truths that were to have set us free. Nor could it ever draw forth the whole of our person because that comes only in making the gift of ourself to another person in the full spontaneity of love. Jesus may have insisted that the Sabbath was made for man, not man for the Sabbath, but the institutional church had become arbiter for personal fulfillment in eternal life.

Coincident with Augustine's appearance upon the church scene, monasticism took hold in Christianity and elevated obedience and chastity to the level of the evangelical counsel of poverty. Monks and members of the various religious orders pronounced vows of perpetual poverty, chastity and obedience. Until recently, those professed of these three vows were considered to be living in the "state of perfection"—a curious concept that left married couples in limbo and the Epistle to the Ephesians on the shelf.

It took homespun Jesuit Karl Rahner to come along with a pert essay that blew the lid off this caboodle of misconceptions. Rahner carefully noted that poverty alone was certainly evangelical, while obedience definitely was not and chastity only doubtfully stipulated as counsels in the Gospel. Rahner was not downgrading religious life but setting things straight as his founder, Ignatius of Loyola, had tried to do four centuries before. This unpretentious Basque had wanted charity to be the sole principle for his order, with practical poverty as its lifestyle. But on edict from the Holy See, Ignatius wrote constitutions for the Jesuit order that still allowed for flexibility in carrying out its various missions.

Contrary to the popular notion, Ignatian obedience is not military but geared to let the superior have the best wisdom at his disposal for making an informed decision. Members are asked to report back to the superior if something occurs to them different from what was commanded, while the superiors can go counter to policy for good reasons. Hardly the lockstep army of Christ as lore of yore had it! So far was

Ignatius from making his order an institution for its own sake that he once stated that if the Pope were to command him to close down the Society, he would need just 15 minutes of prayer in chapel to prepare for dismantling. An 18th-century pope did suppress it but, as heavyweight James J. Corbett put it, "Champions always get off the canvas." Either way it would have been fine with Ignatius, who had only reluctantly let his company get into the business of education. Having attended the University of Paris, he perhaps sensed that educational institutions can sometimes out-Vatican the Vatican in imposing absolute principles.

Ignatius makes but brief mention of chastity, perhaps just to acknowledge that, as a clerical institute in the Roman Church, Jesuits would be bound to celibacy. But Ignatius was no Manichaean. In his *Spiritual Exercises*, his book outlining a series of meditations over 30 days to make a lifetime decision according to the vision of Christ, Ignatius makes much of giving our emotions free play in finding God's goodness in all His beautiful creatures. In keeping with the incredibly open spirit of their founder, 16th-century Jesuits taught that sexual expression outside of marriage was not necessarily a serious sin. Even then, the Jesuits were doing their best to arrest the infection that Augustine had visited upon the Church in its attitude towards the most intimate expression of love. Four centuries later, Jesuits in the U.S.A. were fighting the neo-Manichaeanism put forward by the leading moral theologian at the Catholic University of America. On the eve of the Second Vatican Council, this teacher propagated the notion that couples going steady were committing serious sin! But Jesuit John Connery stemmed the tide with one telling article that simply stated that God in His providence would not make the necessary prelude to the sacrament of marriage the occasion of mortal sin. Contrary to Augustine's dour image that humankind is a *"massa damnata"* (hell-bent populace), the followers of Ignatius follow through on their double belief in the basic goodness of the human nature God's son shares with us and in the effectiveness of His love and grace still welling up in human relationships.

I like to think that the late Cardinal John Dearden of Detroit read the Connery article—because he was a bishop who kept up on his professional reading. The last Sunday in November of 1960 his chancery office had unfortunately ordered that the doctrine condemning "going steady" be preached from every Catholic pulpit in Detroit. Then something amazing happened: Dearden was called to the Second Vatican Council and was put in charge of the section on marriage for the *Pastoral Constitution for the Church in the Modern World.* There he resisted efforts to include statements in that chapter condemning artificial contraception. Some of his clerical friends back in Cleveland were puzzled at his reconsideration of the Catholic teaching on marriage. One attributed it to his listening to his married niece, Kathleen. If that be so, then it is the highest compliment that could be paid him, that a celibate bishop would learn his attitude towards marriage from a married person. Certainly the wisdom contained in the section of the pastoral constitution developed under his guiding hand is a tribute to his courage in turning away from the negative apodictic of the 1960 sermon outline in favor of the incarnational view of the Council document. One of the institutional anomalies of the Roman Church has been that a celibate clergy should lay down the norms for Catholic marriage practice of which they have no direct experience. How refreshing and reassuring the image of this bishop listening to his niece to keep him in touch with the real life married people live. Maybe it was from one of those conversations that an all-important line in the chapter on marriage originated: "Married couples cannot expect that priests have every answer to the moral questions that arise in marriage."[2] This is a sympathetic echo over four centuries from those Jesuit moral theologians who insisted that sexuality was good and that its expression outside of marriage was not necessarily a serious sin.

This has been the most sensitive and far-reaching intrusion that the institutional church has made: to make sexuality wrong except within the context of legitimate marriage. John Macmurray picks up on the inadequacy of this norm in an incisive statement: "Real personal love is the basis in the absence of which specifically sexual relations are unchaste and immoral. This holds inside marriage just as much as outside it."[3] A girl who marries a man for his money but has no love for him as a person may have her marriage blessed in church but this does not save her from being immoral. There can also be a couple living together who are devoted to one another with all the love they can give but shy away from the marriage ceremony because of the unhappy home life each had suffered because of divorce in both of their families. It would be difficult to call their situation immoral because at that stage neither can risk repeating the domestic horrors that life before their parents' divorce had brought them.

The more radical inadequacy is the very attitude towards sexuality that makes it suspect until the honeymoon. This has been the devastating legacy of the Augustinian viewpoint on marriage. Instead of teaching sexuality as something good and part of our integrity as a human person, the Church over the centuries has managed to separate it from the principle of love of which it can be the most intimate expression. Much better to teach our young that sexuality is good and always has been but that certain contexts in expressing sexuality can be contrary to the principle of love for which it stands. Ironically, with the advent of the contraceptive pill, full attention can now be given to the goodness of sexual expression in itself without its being overshadowed by neighborhood condemnation of a girl's having a child born out of wedlock. One wonders whether if in the past there wasn't more concern about who would look after the child born of the "illegitimate" union than about the actual morality of love that conceived the child. In any case, it is a must that our good young people don't have to do a complete changeabout in their perception of their sexuality on the eve of their wedding. Equally serious, however, is the separation of love from sexual expression that so many of our movies, video- cassettes and novels consider to be par for the course. This is another cultural institution—the media—that has to be dealt with. But, the Christian churches still have to bear the brunt of responsibility for having made sexual abstention a virtue at the expense of the full personal engagement of love in marriage.

Not only has this curbed personal spontaneity through an external norm. Such turning in on self through asceticism can make a person individualistic, as Macmurray remarks in a shrewd observation:

> Its effect is to produce a concentration of the self upon itself. The individual self becomes the central problem; its impulses and demands are the constant preoccupation of the mind . . . But the effort to suppress the self will disappear and the demand for self-fulfillment will take its place. The negative individualism which suppression had created will manifest itself as a positive individualism.[4]

Macmurray touches upon the elemental reason why institutional conformity can never be an image that engages the whole of oneself: When we pare ourselves down to the model the institution prescribes, we go on the defensive with an interior groan that says "This is a hell of a note—I'm not allowed to be myself." In giving full scope to my spontaneous delight in the world I experience as part of it, institution calls me out of order if my actions and expressions don't match the preset mold. But my interior spirit still says "Malarkey." The institution implies that in being true to my unique self, I am wrong. And my pent-up individuality finally exclaims, "If that be so I'll get out of your way and go on my own."

Down deep within each of us, there is a sense of God-given worth that is an implicit act of faith in God's providence and in the twin truths of the Incarnation and Redemption. Furthermore, it is not the spontaneous expression of self that turns us individualistic. For what is most personal about ourselves is our unique spirit of love that gives itself away to the beloved. What gives rise to the individualistic streak within us is being put on the defensive by the institution. Macmurray alludes to this in a very honest remark about celibacy:

> It is not the abstinence from sexual expression that is the root of the trouble, but making this an end in itself. Then it becomes an expression of negative self-centeredness; of the desire to be superior to one's own nature, which can only rise from a sense of inferiority; of the will to save one's own life by which one loses it.[5]

This small paragraph speaks volumes because it cuts right to the cancer that the Manichaean contagion has visited upon Christianity.

Abstention from sexual expression has value only in the deeper love that prompts it. Celibacy is not a virtue. Chastity in Macmurray's fine definition of it is the emotional sincerity without which no expression of love can be true. It is out of this deeper love for his wife back home that an Army lieutenant overseas turns away from the opportunity for sexual expression with this beautiful German girl he has come to know.

It is out of this same deeper love that the young Wall Street accountant decides not to go to bed with the girlfriend who yearns to express her love for him physically. She may feel that she is not sexually attractive to him. If that were the case, he would not have to invoke his deeper love for her. Of course he is attracted to her—that's what had him overcome the shyness behind his suave manner to go up and introduce himself in the first place. But the spontaneity of his initial love for her just hasn't taken root in a more profound friendship. As much as she might want sexual union with him, he is not a liar. He will not make love with a girl he knows he will not be seeing much of in the future.

Oh, in college he read the Philip Roth repartee—humorous and brassy in depicting its heroes—but just as insensitive and dishonest. No, he will not inflict the hurt of participating in sexual activity with a girl he knows he will eventually leave—even if that is what she desires at the moment. This would give a value to sexual expression it doesn't have and would be in a sense just as wayward as the taboo against sexual expression. Personal love does not hinge upon anatomy. Separated from sincere love, both abstention and indulgence become values unto themselves and not integrated into a person's character. He doesn't know when the time will come when sexual love will be for him an honest expression of sincere friendship. But in the meantime, his deeper love for this refreshing companion dissuades him from the charade of going to bed with her as if there were a mutual commitment of ongoing love.

He is not being pious. He has seen the hurt on the faces of too many personable girls moping around from the latest letdown. He refuses to be another gallant who is all charm and promise but whose word is rendezvous candlewax. It saddens him that these girls once· so full of hopes for their future have settled for the less than honest love offered to them. But in this age of skin-deep skin-game cassettes, the dull thud of the disco beat has drummed out a sense of interior worth in too many attractive people his age. He is not trying to clean up Manhattan; he just can't stand the dishonesty of it all—no wonder Roth has escaped to his Connecticut refuge—and half chuckles at their trying to be so awfully authentic, hanging out in bars and getting soused at four in the morning. With friends? How can you call somebody a friend you met yesterday! Close acquaintance maybe, but not friend! That is one word that has to keep its meaning. But, maybe the loose usage is more hope than desperation. He knows that all each of them really wants is for someone to care—really to care for them.

Yes, that's what we all want: home on Your welcoming shoulder. We don't know when or where we may find it once we leave our parental homestead to go off on our own for good. That 'for good' remains a question mark that becomes an exclamation point in those sunny moments of true friendship that one can discern perhaps only from the vantage point of years. Yet searching with hindsight is a contradiction. The appreciation of a sincere friendship is a matter of insight that knows no age or timetable. Foresight, by contrast, is often an alias for a prudence certified only from hindsight. And too much attention to individual security out of prudence seals off fresh horizons for personal fulfillment that involve risk. Prudence is someone else's hindsight that can blur a person's own insight.

Movie star Betty Hutton didn't find home until after she had gone through several marriages and several millions. Just as the Samaritan woman in John's account had found home on the welcoming shoulder of Jesus—and I have no doubt at all that the ease of release from the burden of her years came on the same shoulder that the Gospel author had leaned upon at the last supper—Betty Hutton had found it on the shoulder of the priest who welcomed her as housekeeper at a Catholic rectory in Rhode Island. No wonder my mom and dad didn't complain about marriage in a rectory. The rectory was part of something greater—the plus side of church as institution. It was always "there," like the home of the prodigal son with the father looking down the road awaiting his return. The elder brother's "foresight" foreclosed his risking to ask his Dad if he could celebrate belonging with his own friends. His prudence was so stuffy that he thought he could earn security by obeying orders and doing his job. His father's home had become so institutional for the elder brother that his father had to come outside to say: "Hey son, you are always with me and everything I have is yours, but we had to celebrate because your brother was lost and has come home." (Lk. 15:32)

Betty Hutton's marriages were not failures simply because they didn't last. This woman's middle name was spontaneity and I'm sure that she took the risk of total gift in each relationship because, as she bubbled in the movie musical, "You can't get a man with a gun." There were moments of friendship in those marriages and her grandchildren of today stir her memory of them. The Rhode Island priest never talked of her mistakes because sincere searching is never a mis-

take. And Jesus merely mentioned the Samaritan woman's five pre-
vious marriages and live-in lover to break the ice of her cool aplomb.
He just wanted to let her know that in the risk of gift she was being
true to herself, and the lack of permanent response even five times
over did not depreciate her own worth. He himself took the risk of
friendship with Judas. Jesus even invited him to the Last Supper
knowing he was conniving with the Temple coterie for a doublecross.
Not much foresight there, and Jesus was abandoned on Calvary as a
result. No— the only foresight Jesus ever spoke of was the leap of
total love that is all risk.

The greatest tribute to the Church is that, for all its institutional
encrustations, you still find among its Catholic, Protestant and Orthodox clergy, ministers who really live this kindness of Christ. On the
PBS television show that was her sole return to the spotlight, Betty
Hutton was all tears of gratitude for the priest in the audience who had
taken her in when she was down and out. That same sense of welcome is described by Alec Guinness in his autobiography, *Blessings in
Disguise.* He was on location in France doing a "Father Brown"
movie and found it easier to go to the auberge for lunch still dressed
in his cassock. A little French boy came up and nonchalantly put his
hand in that of the actor, who answered the *"Bonjour, mon Pére"* in a
bit of a grunt since *bonjour* and *merci* were the extent of his French.
The lad babbled away as they shared the roadway, with Alec giving
the knowing nod that covered his ignorance of all but the youngster's
complete trust in the representative of the Church. As the boy said his
"Au revoir" at his gate, Guinness—himself an illegitimate child—realized why Church was a "blessing in disguise," after his book title.
There was always someone beyond the family abode whom a person
could call Father.

I used to think that the Protestant sects that objected to the Anglican and Roman churches calling their clerics "Father" had a point.
Now I'm not so sure. I was confusing the unfortunate separation of
laity and clergy with the title "Father," which doesn't imply separation
at all. Rather does it mean welcome from a particular person who
represents the Church.

We need a haven beyond our house so we don't make our own
fathers God. Each of us needs to be responsible to someone, to have a
sense of acceptance from someone. That first someone was our Dad.

Present or absent, he is our progenitor and we need his acceptance early or late. But he isn't perfect—never pretended to be. He took charge of us simply because he was our father. Remember the song from *Carousel*, "My Boy Bill," with its wonderful Hammerstein insight that a man can be a pal to his son but he has to be a father to his daughter. Every daughter I've ever met will tell you that it's true, even when she goes her independent way in the full enthusiasm of young womanhood. In the movie, *Reunion at Fairboro*, Robert Mitchum's newfound (after 20 years) granddaughter exclaims, "I think you need somebody to look after you." She was also speaking her own need.

When Dad and Mom take us to church to acknowledge that God is our father—and, if Catholic, introduce the minister as "Father"— something good happens. I know I have a haven beyond my household. And if some sad day my father is taken from me in a car crash or the trauma of divorce, I still have in God someone to whom I am responsible and accountable. I can also take my gripes about God and religion to the parish "Father." Should he become a pain or stubborn or plainly wrong, I can dispense with him. If, however, I have made my own father God, I can disagree with him but cannot dispense with him. I will spend a lifetime trying to gain his approval because I have no God except him. But if I live in the knowledge that I'm accountable to God the Father who reads my heart and says I'm OK, then any misunderstanding I might have with my dad will not threaten my worth as a person. My sense of belonging ultimately rests with God— as does my dad's. So, he and I can pray together to the same God and don't have to prove ourselves in each other's eyes.

Such deep-down belief in God as father (or as mother) can also save us from the trap of individualism. For, as G.K. Chesterton once said, "Self-made men bear the defects of their creators." His near-contemporary, John Macmurray, was more vehement: "The great negation of religion is individualism, egocentricity become a philosophy; and it is inherently atheist, however much it says 'Lord, Lord!'"[6] If God smiles— and his Incarnate Son Jesus certainly must have when young Mark lost his shirt in escaping the temple police (Mark 14:56)—it must be at the self-assured atheist. Such a person's need to be heard implies some kind of relationship with others. When that bond has been woven over the years with a beloved friend or spouse, he weeps at her death. No, he's not just an individual; he has been participant in a relationship so close as to cause tears at her passing. He has already experienced God at the heart of this relationship. How else explain that this confirmed individualist would let go of his self-interest enough to give himself away in forming the deep bond with his beloved.

The atheist's demand to be heard may simply be what St-Ex points to as the basic need we each have—to be acknowledged! An atheist's rejection of God may go back to a dismal experience with representatives of the church at a very sensitive time in his life—the death of a parent or his own wedding. Put on the defensive, he became the individualist who would insist upon being recognized without letting anyone ever get close enough to reject him again. However much he may declaim that a good God could never permit the evil of extermination camps, the real evil for him is not to have been acknowledged by a churchman or maybe his dad! So, perhaps the best way to get past his rhetoric to his own truth is simply to ask, "How's your Dad?" His answer may be: well, he died some years ago. No matter—Dad as the first authority figure in our life holds most of the aces about our self-acceptance. Mom's hand is a royal flush—in hearts!

We're back home again, but only in our dreams? No—in that reservoir of memory and early impressions that still color the basic image we each make of ourselves as persons. Where does this search for our personal significance and fulfillment take us? Anne Morrow Lindbergh answers simply—"Within."

- 3 -

Knowing You—
Knowing Me

IF THERE'S PROVIDENCE IN A NAME, THEN FOR MRS. LINDBERGH TO BE
Anne is *neat*—nice! For from early Christian times, Anne has stood
for mother after Mary's own. The French had the good sense to call
their cathedrals Notre Dame, our Lady—not Notre Mère. That title is
Anne's. So, you'll find images of mother Anne all round France, one
of the best in the Louvre thanks to Leonardo DiVinci's Anne is the
picture of a youthful grandmother with lad Jesus resting on her knee.
And only a young grandmother like Anne Lindbergh could write *Gift
from the Sea*,[1] the classic of the feminist era. Ms. Steinem may get
the glory and Ms. Freidan the billing; but Mrs. Lindbergh's book has
been time-tested over 33 years. She keeps in the background, true to
Yeats' praise of playwright Synge for having enough self-assurance
not to be self-assertive.

That's where Anne Lindbergh leads us—to the center of our personal worth. She knows the way from the joys and sorrows—flowers
and nettles is her description—she has carried as wife, daughter, sister,
friend, and mother to five children, after the tragic death of her first-
born. (The death of a firstborn is the sword through the heart of Mary
that Simeon presaged. Even in her 80th year, my own mother found it
difficult to speak about her firstborn who died of carcinoma at the age
of a year and a half. After Mom's death, I had prints made from an
old negative of the happy threesome from Dixon, Illinois: Mom, Dad,

and Patricia. None of us five who came later could ever replace Patricia—all blessing to her smiling memory.) Anne Morrow Lindbergh gathers her wisdom in a "few shells"—her symbols for the shifting phases we go through in searching for personal fulfillment. What's your favorite "beach" for quiet reflection? Anne Lindbergh's was a rented cottage on an island off the west coast of Florida. My treasured spot is Grace Kelly's garden near the port of Monaco. I was lucky enough to spend an afternoon in the *roseraie* her husband planted in her memory. It was the first day of October and the tourists were elsewhere. I was alone in this garden set out with fresh varieties of roses encircling the sculpture of the dear lady from Philadelphia. It was good to be there, if only to savor St-Ex's line: "When cross-breeding produces a new rose in a garden, all the gardeners are excited."[2] The new rose nearest Grace's profile is called Princess of Monaco.

The rose has become my preferred symbol because of Saint Exupéry's insight that "It's the time you squander upon your rose that makes your rose so special"[3]—the rose being the beloved in the heart of each of us. He or she is part of the double question that comes up in the solitude of a garden or beach reflection: Who is the beloved with whom you would like "to expend" priceless moments and what would you love to do to find yourself completely? Searching for personal fulfillment goes on for life—whether its symbol is Anne Lindbergh's moonshell or Princess Grace's October rose. The sound of the ever-present ocean in a seashell reminds us that the only time action knows is "now" and the bud beneath the mature flower suggests our recurring urge to begin again.

That need was the theme of Robert Preston's last film. Preston was Finnegan and his philosophy was the movie title: *Finnegan Begin Again*. So, when the 40-year-old divorcée, played by Mary Tyler Moore, asks Finnegan, "Are you really 65?" he preens with full Preston aplomb—"I don't understand it myself!" Grace is gone these 12 years past and the "Music Man" for seven (1987); but both are ageless because they were always so alive and witty. Recall Grace's response to Albert Hitchcock who had deliberately repeated an off-color story within her hearing and then wryly asked, "Did I embarrass you?" Her quick comeback: "Oh no, Mr. Hitchcock; I went to a convent school and heard all your stories before I was 13." Or to Marlon Brandon the moment the two had become the youngest to receive the Oscar for best actress/actor: "I think it is the gentleman who is supposed to kiss the lady." But I remember Grace for her lines inscribed on a rock in her garden: "What is so special about a rose that it seems far more than a flower? Perhaps it is the mystery it has gathered through the ages. Perhaps it is the joy that it continues to give." My memory of Robert Preston rests in one line from the scene in *The Music Man* with young Winthrop. Preston has been found out as tone-deaf and con-artist, so eight-year-old Winthrop confronts him in tears: "You don't know how to play an instrument, do you?" "No" is the "professor's" honest reply. Winthrop's follow-up: "So you don't have a band." Robert Preston answers for all of us, "Kid, I think I *always* have a band." We always have an image of the person each of us is striving to become, even if we falter along the way. Without this dream there is no star for our searching, whether in a garden or along a seashore. It is this image of fulfillment that we seek to clarify as we set aside the press of duty for our walk in the garden or along the strand.

Anne's initial chapter entitled "Channelled Whelk" is about getting ready to search out our "star." I used to think you could simply "go for it," but that was before I had to negotiate Newark, JFK or LaGuardia airports just to get away. If Anne Lindbergh had to fly out of LaGuardia to get to her Florida retreat, I'm sure it took her the whole trip down to unwind. It was much more relaxing when she and her husband were plotting the Pacific routes for PanAm in the open cockpits of their seaplane. Making the time to get away is the best start. And leaving wardrobe and portable telephone behind is a must. As Anne remarks in that refreshing first chapter, it is amazing how much we can do without in terms of carpeting and cutlery if we really do want to be away on our own. But just as the channelled whelk symbolizes the shedding of external hazards to getting inside oneself, the moonshell encompasses the interior corners that have to be cleared to find personal peace.

Awareness is what we want: open horizons, nothing barred. In a real sense we get away neither to work on private projects nor to rest our weary bones. This would put purpose to our search and confine our focus to that purpose. For then we're occupied, preoccupied, and have thwarted the chance to find our full self. No, this time you don't have to bring back photos to prove you were on vacation. You don't ask for a receipt at the tollgate as you drive your Avis towards the sea. We each have become such a network of reflexes in our complex society. We even have "communications systems!" Little wonder our divorce rate is so high—we're not in touch with the other at all but only with her programmed "answering machine." So we have to swing free of systems, especially the fears that are built into our own system.

What fears? Well, mainly the fear of what I might find out if I take a careful look at what is really important to me at the heart of my being. Then, sincerity would require that I act upon it. That's John Macmurray: "All meaningful knowledge is for the sake of action."[4] That's Antoine de Saint Exupéry: "You are revealed in your action: this is your true identity."[5] And, yes, that's my Dad. When he went in to ask his boss for a raise, he felt that his record with the Medusa Cement Company was so clear that if he were turned down he must leave the firm. The boss evidently got the message and my dad the raise. This is the only life we will ever lead so we must, not from an external norm but from inner integrity, live according to what we know to be true for ourselves.

But we're afraid of losing our job, not being accepted in the neighborhood, hurting our friends or letting people down if we go ahead and do what we know is best. Anne Lindbergh reminds us that only sincere friends belong in our home, and who's to tell what the right job is for us. Remember the glut of unemployed engineers after Neil Armstrong had reached the moon. One of them started an ice-cream stand and enjoyed it so much more than mission control. He finally had a chance to spend time with his family, with a couple of his children working with him.

Fear does crowd a careful look at our own world of experience—the fear of disapproval from our elders or companions, should we let our spontaneous response to the fresh vistas of possibility engaging our unique spirit run counter to accepted goals. Our key institutions, the schools and the churches, have prescribed those purposes for us so insistently that we block out our awareness of those dimensions of the world that don't fit the prescription or the purpose. The purpose of church education is to make us good before God and humankind; the purpose of school education is to make us skilled on the job and responsible in the neighborhood. The ethic church puts across is that of the good person which gives us a sense of self-satisfaction if we live true to that model. This fits in comfortably with the plan of society which requires the proper deportment and efficient performance that our schools are designed to develop. The upshot is that our open awareness of the world through aesthetic appreciation of its beauty, goodness and possibilities for personal spontaneity is constricted. No wonder Anne Lindbergh gets us to the beach and Grace of Monaco to a rose garden—we can become aware of our unique significance only through sensitive awareness. Macmurray is forthright about this:

> For the determination of values we are dependent on our emotions—or on those of someone else . . . There can be no hope of educating our emotions unless we stop relying on other people's for our judgments of value. We must learn to feel for ourselves, even if we make mistakes.[6]

So, we put the fear of being wrong or incorrect behind us as we take a careful look at our own identity—with hints from Anne Lindbergh, who doesn't mind if we disagree with her as long as it is our own felt experience. That is our inner peace—being true to our unique self. This for a woman is total gift! And for all of us—since what is unique about each of us is our capacity for total gift to another. What disturbs the serenity of women is the sense that their gift lacks significance, perhaps for not being appreciated or even received. This after all is what we all seek in life: personal significance in and through the relationships created through mutual gift. British psychologist Harry Guntrip, who embraced John Macmurray's notion of person, concurs: "Our psychology must begin with the human being striving to become actually what he or she is potentially, a significant person related in meaningful ways to other persons."[7] Anne Lindbergh puts this beautifully in speaking of the inner harmony that comes of giving oneself completely and being received completely. But there's the rub—the ultimate fear we have to deal with. It's the misgiving that in making total gift to another, he or she will rebuff me and deprive me of inner peace. Anne does speak of a woman going to God to make this dedication in the assurance that her gift will be accepted unconditionally. True enough in a profound way—but going to God doesn't quite face up to the fear of rejection or misunderstanding from the person who means most to me here on earth. But have I really come to know my beloved or have I stopped short? For, to borrow from Tennessee Williams, "It's almost impossible for anybody to believe they're not loved by someone they believe they love."[8] We cannot let the prospect of being let down keep us from coming to know our beloved. Otherwise our friendship is based on fantasy and never was.

The question is three-dimensional. First, I must be sure that I really know myself and that I really know my best friend to whom I would make total gift. Anne Lindbergh speaks of the elation we feel in that initial experience of uncluttered friendship that she calls "Double Sunrise." Strange that we should call this love "romantic" since Roman Stoicism was so wary of our emotions getting in the way of "mature" decisions and action. We speak of people being "in love" as if it were a stage people go through until they get back to the solid reality of the workaday world. Rome lent out its adjective with a small "r" well aware that its rational policy would carry the day. This imperialism extended even to the wedding day—with its arranged marriages to keep the ruling families entwined with appropriate offspring. We still feel for Rod Steiger's "Marty," as written for TV by Paddy Chayefsky. The 30ish Bronx Italian butcher has finally found a girlfriend, who happens to be of British descent. So the neighborhood matrons descend upon him, "But Marty—she's not Italian!" That finest half-hour on television ends with Marty putting Rome in the form of Little Italy behind him as he phones the one girl who is delighted to receive his total gift. Marty knew he was right. Yes, he was bowled over, as Grace Kelly was when she won the Oscar and Prince Ranier proposed to her.

These moments are golden—and summon up all the elation and élan from the depths of our being. Of course the moment is emotional—and all the more true for that. Weddings are emotional, and funerals are emotional, and baptisms are emotional and Christmas is emotional. Deeply so. That's my point: profound appreciation of the worth of another human being and therefore of oneself is not a first-blush reaction; it is intuitive appraisal or, better, emotional appreciation arising from the unique spirit of one human responding to the unique spirit of another.

John Macmurray unflinchingly supports the soundness of this knowledge of another: "Objective emotion is not a mere reaction to a stimulus. It is an immediate appreciation of the value and significance of real things."[9] The focus, however, must be on the reality of the other if mine is to be real love for him or her and not just self-satisfaction or infatuation.

Coming to know the other and oneself in relation to the other is not a matter of prudence, but of intuitive tact—being in touch with the reality of the other. Tact, not tactics, for these would be the means to an end prudence dictates. And that would trap us in our own logic. Responding to another, as St-Ex insists, has nothing to do with goals and strategies—it is a movement of one's spirit.[10] The approach of love reveals the person, while tact discerns whether she wants your company just now or would rather be on her own. If you start clinging to her or burdening her with appointments to keep, it is no longer love but tactless clutching. You no longer allow her the space to choose you in full spontaneity as her friend. The late Nat "King" Cole poignantly phrases this outcome in his song, *"When I Fall in Love,"* with the regret that in our unsettled world love succumbs before it ever has a chance to take root.

This is the chagrin that Philip Roth has his hero face at the end of *Goodbye, Columbus.* After rollicking times with his girlfriend, Neil gets very serious about mistaking sexual clutching for love in his quest to find personal fulfillment in relationship with another:

> What was it inside me that had turned pursuit and clutching into love, and then turned it inside out again? What was it that had turned winning into losing, and losing—who knows—into winning? I was sure I had loved Brenda, though standing there, I knew I couldn't any longer. And I knew it would be a long while before I made love to anyone else the way I made love to her. With anyone else could I summon up such a passion? Whatever spawned my love for her, had that spawned such lust too? If she had only been slightly *not* Brenda . . . but then would I have loved her? I looked hard at the image of me . . .[11]

There isn't any facile answer to Roth's question that has haunted our young (and not so young) people since the marriage choice was placed entirely in their hands. It may be a failure in trust. Anne Lindbergh suggests at the very beginning of *Gift from the Sea* that you must wait upon the other's timing to let her reveal herself as person and as friend. We cannot impose our timetable or our preconceived notion of "girl-friend" upon her. Maybe that was Neil's mistake, and Brenda's. They each had this notion about how a girl/man is to be had. But a true friend is never "had"! Even if the girl desires to be possessed and sexually fulfilled, there comes a time when she wants "out," unless she trusts herself to be worthy of friendship. Otherwise her readiness for sexual expression with this boy she is fond of could signal her misgiving that "when he comes to know the real me, he will leave me; so we'll keep this involvement at a mutually-acceptable level by going to bed with one another." Sexual intimacy camouflages her fear of becoming too close to another personally. Harry Guntrip goes to the heart of the matter:

> When we fail to achieve genuinely personal relationships, if we do not retreat from human contacts, we may substitute appetitive gratifications instead, and then the appetitive compulsion symbolizes our reaching out after personal relationship, as is conspicuously the case in sexual compulsions. It is the individual who is inwardly isolated from other people, who has no genuine flow of sympathetic, friendly feeling towards others, who cannot really love, who is driven in desperation to clutch at physical contact to make up for inability to achieve emotional rapport. If, on the other hand, such an individual has inhibited all emotional response and physical impulse with it, he may fall back on purely intellectual intercourse which is impersonal and concerned with ideas rather than with people. One can argue and discuss with people with whom one has nothing really in common, but if one has little capacity for having "something in common" with other folk, then intellectual interests may give an illusory sense of still maintaining human contacts. Depersonalized physical and depersonalized intellectual intercourse should rank equally as betrayals of true human living, as substitutes for genuine personal relationship.[12]

Harry Guntrip faces this human dilemma whole. He talks about young people like Neil who fail to find lasting friendship with someone they love, perhaps through premature sexual intimacy. But at least they took the risk of involvement with another in a search for relationship. Unlike those others who stand aside and critique the "loose living" of young adults in university seminars, while inwardly fearful of a close relationship with anyone. No wonder Jesus felt comfortable in talking with the Samaritan woman because at least she had taken risks in her searching and got right to the point in conversation. Maybe Neil and Brenda had never had a true conversation—that turning towards the other in a listening way. Conversation is not so much a matter of talk as of giving oneself away unreservedly instead of keeping to oneself. This may mean driving a hundred miles without a word being said in the simple assurance of being at the side of your friend who needs to rest in her thoughts just now. "It's the time that you squander upon your rose that makes your rose so special."

This brings us to the second dimension of genuine knowledge of the other. Do I accept her just as she is? Do I acknowledge her faults or, as the Irish say so delicately, "allow her the defects of her qualities?" For built into our personalities are our mannerisms and small "hang-ups," those kinesthetic reactions engrained since youth—like the compulsion to pick up any article of clothing lying on the floor. (Jean Kerr's way of dealing with screams erupting from her boys' room was to shout: "Hang up your pants." The pause in the brawl invariably went for a good cause.) There will come a day when you will have to face up to all the peculiar characteristics in your beloved—the day your chin hits the cement, so to say, and you come up muttering: "Is she really like that?" "Uh-huh" (Yes.) "Is she likely to change?" "Huh-uh" (NO.) "Do you still love her?" "Of course!" In fact, that day of disillusionment is the day you really begin to love your beloved for herself and not simply delight in your cherished image of her. It's a mistake to put a woman on a pedestal because this is not treating her as an equal. Your friend wants you to accept her and love her as she is. The French maxim rings true: *"Leur marquer trop de respect, c'est aussi leur manquer de respect"*—"To show women too much respect is to lack respect for them." John Macmurray gives us a deeper reason why: "If you love a person, you love him or her in their stark reality and refuse to shut your eyes to their defects and errors. For to do that is to shut your eyes to their needs."[13] The test of love is affirming your beloved in her total reality as she is. To idealize her, even in praising her, stifles the relationship.

The third dimension in reaching the full reality of your friend and of yourself in relationship to her is contained in an insight of Anne Lindbergh's. You cannot hold either yourself or your beloved to one moment in a relationship. People change. You will change and she will change and your relationship will take on different forms. Hopefully it will deepen and become richer; or maybe it will fade. Anne Lindbergh suggests that there can be continuity in a relationship but never in the same form. The glowing experiences in the first discovery of the other in friendship cannot last. Friendship takes root in sharing. But this involves accommodation to the friend's preferences and timetable and job obligations. So soon does the relationship of friendship depend upon reciprocal give-and-take. If either party does not wish to be encumbered, the very use of that term calls the relationship into question almost at the outset. It could be mere delight in the refreshing company of the other without it ever being mutual love. One or other may wish that the relationship would last but again the choice must be mutual and cannot be forced or earned.

If, blessedly, a couple come to know each other in an open and honest way and each becomes the person the other would like to spend a lifetime with, they settle into marriage. Home is each other's welcoming shoulder, but cooperation is necessary if they are to run a household. The efforts they make in the common venture of married friendship is their way of showing love for one another, boring as doing laundry can be. This could be what Saint Exupéry meant in his line from *Terre des hommes*: "Love is not gazing at each other—it is looking at the world over each other's shoulder."[14] The couple have moved from the "double sunrise" of spontaneous lunches or afternoon walks on a mountain trail. They are immersed in the round of routine activity on the job or back home that Anne Lindbergh dubs the "Oyster Bed." In appearance household chores and care for husband and children can be drab, but hidden therein is the "pearl of great price," to use Jesus' expression for personal fulfillment. I like the single pearl a bride sometimes wears as her wedding necklace. It is a fine symbol for all the "oyster bed" shopping, cooking and running to hospital emergency rooms her mom and dad went through to bring her to this sparkling moment in her life. And if her name is Margaret, all the more appropriate—her very name means "pearl."

Speaking of "moments" brings up the reason Anne Lindbergh gives for not clinging to the "double sunrise" phase of friendship and for not pinning your friend to that early stage of your relationship. Anne speaks of life being a series of present moments, some of which we naturally keep in fond memory. She even suggests that it is a fine idea for a couple to take a break together, even if it is just a weekend away, to celebrate once again the glowing motivation that first brought them together as friends and then spouses. The reason they now appreciate that initial encounter is the providential shape it gave to their lives.

Yes, Providence. I believe in divine providence—not chance. Else I would not have survived the broken neck I sustained when scaffolding fell on me during the Manhattan parade for our 1984 Olympians. And there's the greater providence that leads you to those particular persons who have enriched your life. Part of this belief in providence is not to fix your friend at any one stage in your relationship. For this has a double detriment. First, it doesn't allow your friend to grow as a person in response to your care for her in the relationship. The other hazard is that you no longer are keeping aware of your friend, but are delighting in the early image you cherish of her at the ripe old age of 20 when you first met her. So, back in the moonshell again, do you have the inner peace that gladly says, "My beloved has blossomed like a rose," even if that has meant that she has less time to spend with you because of certain needs that are important to her? Do you encourage her to go through a new door, now that the earlier stages of your relationship and certain shared responsibilities have become history?

Mrs. Lindbergh has the wonderful insight to suggest that functions should be shed when they are no longer functional. Functions serve the friendship, not the other way around. When the children are ready to leave home, we set them free, as we insisted that our parents do in our regard. The ambush of ambition that has us marry our job is a subtle way of identifying with a function that is less than ourselves and keeps us from going through a new door.

Anne and Charles Lindbergh were always ready to support each other in going through new doors. They had been doing that since he took her on her first airplane ride. That is perhaps the finest part of her book, where she speaks of the risk of going through a new door in the afternoon of life. She puts to rest the usual chestnut that a person who makes a drastic change in his or her life is suffering from middle-age crisis. She rightly pinpoints the truth that searching is a lifelong venture which is the sign of personal growth. Perhaps the greatest encouragement we can give our young friends in their search for happiness and personal fulfillment is to take the risk ourselves to new phases in our own living. What saddens me most is to see once-energetic men sitting on mall benches wearing their baseball caps. The caps are symbolic of the youth they lost when they were forcibly retired at 65 and now have to do the senior citizen bit. What a contrast to *Der Alte,* Konrad Adenauer who did not become Chancellor of West Germany until he was 75 and retired at 88!

We must always be ready to go through new doors and support our best friend in her growth as a person. Anne Lindbergh likens this to a dance in which we don't cling to our partner nor possess her but attend to her as we keep the harmony of our life together. I'm sure that the reason my students delight in her book written a generation ago is that her counsel for women (and men) who have reached the sunny side of 50 (sunup or sundown) is just as pertinent for them in their search for personal fulfillment. Robert Preston was ever young, and Grace of Monaco was ever young, and Anne Lindbergh is ever young because in being true to their inner selves they let their lifelong friends, their spouses, go through new doors with a lilt in their walk. A dance—Preston's was a skip that wished sweet dreams to his wife, Grace's was a waltz with Ranier at the Rose Ball for their Monaco hospital, and Anne's was a stroll on the Maui seashore with her Charles. Just after her "double sunrise" moment of first meeting the famous aviator, Anne had written her sister, "He is hopelessly logical and such a dear." Anne knew her beloved. She had the right attitude.

- 4 -
Three Attitudes

IF CLOTH COULD KEEP, FUTURE ARCHAEOLOGISTS COULD LEARN THE lore of our day from slogans on our T-shirts. One I saw a Manhattan girl wearing read, "I have an attitude." I liked that because we all do. In fact, we have three basic attitudes or perspectives we take towards the world, especially the world of other people: the functional perspective, the appreciation perspective and the personal perspective. John Macmurray once said that we approach other people to use them, admire them or worship them. Perhaps too succinct because it seems to leave out keeping some at bay. He would answer that merely using people or admiring them cordons them off. Worship? Too strong unless there's someone I love who is always in my mind and heart. Worship need not mean adoration. It simply means making someone besides myself the most important person in my living, and God doesn't mind if that's your fiancé. John's 1st Epistle cleared that up long ago: "No one has ever seen God; but if we love one another, God abides in us and his love is perfected in us." (1 John 4:12) That's the passage in Scripture I live by because I'm blessed in those who occupy a corner of my heart always. So do our young dating couples, but why do so many adults get distracted? Perhaps it hinges upon that unwritten line etched in their spirit: "I have an attitude!" For if the controlling attitude or perspective a person takes towards others is functional or pragmatic, he or she will never get to know other people as they are.

We tend to adopt an attitude towards others in terms of those images of acceptance that have been instilled in us. If we have been molded in a context which puts a premium upon performing well, we

41

will tend to view others the same way. This shapes the functional perspective. We have seen how our schools and churches do this without letup. Discipline we all need in order to get on well with others. But the stars behind our names on the charts at school have nothing to do with St-Ex's star that symbolizes our search for personal fulfillment. Nor with Myles Connolly's that stands for our unique worth as persons:

> You always says: Poor me, what can I do?
> Good heavens, child, just think of what you are!
> Why scorn the sky for being merely blue
> Or spurn a star for being just a star?[1]

The school stars come in various colors for comparison's sake. Individual performance is judged against the records of others, as if schooling were the Olympic games. (Should the best student in Ken's chemistry class get "D," the scientist invokes the "hay-stack curve" for grading. Leave it to the "scientific" mind to come up with a formula allowing only a certain percentage of a class to merit an "A." The hypothesis that intelligence is parceled out in percentiles is pabulum!]

This competition for marks follows us right into the marketplace where our salaries and raises are set according to our performance ratings. In our "bottom-line" times of profit and loss, an individual's worth comes down to his or her financial benefit to a firm—this year! (Chesterton may have been right: he says we are trained to be accountants from the crib where we pushed the colored shish kebab counters from one end of the rod to the other.) Management's attitude is coldly pragmatic and is blind to the contribution the individual has made to the company over the years in personal initiative, creativity, and extra hours on the job.

This functional attitude is what Harry Curry has to confront in son Noah in N. Richard Nash's *The Rainmaker*. The play is set on the Curry ranch in the drought-ridden Kansas of the 30s. With cattle dying and income shrinking, foreman Noah has laid off the two farm hands. Harry (H.C.) is upset with his son for this because these two workers are persons, not figures. But H.C.'s deeper difficulty with Noah is that he brings this functional attitude into the house. It is Noah's controlling viewpoint. The *functional perspective* implicitly says, "*You are acceptable to me for my use or for my delight.*" This is

well and good at work but has nothing to do with home and friendship.

Noah fits right in with the U.S. managerial style of the 80s and
90s. His "bottom-line" attitude prevails, even as the dollar slides this
winter of '92-93. Necessary for the marketplace, but not inside the
Curry home that includes Liz and Jim. H.C. is a widower who is concerned about his daughter who is in her late 20s with no immediate
prospect for marriage. Noah's functional attitude is bluntly blurted
when he tells Liz that if she's to be married she has to get a man the
"way a man is had," and that this will be almost impossible for her
since she is "plain." (So absolutely tactless as to be "imprudent" even
by the Stoic standards of the Romans.)

Noah's functional attitude is blind to beauty because its logic
bars emotional appreciation of another's unique spirit. Yet, even in
our own time, many a girl feels that she has to live up to the "sexy"
image she has been led to believe is all that counts with men. "That's
how a man is to be had." And it is true that many a man wants the
company of an attractive girl for his own delight. But then he's not
really in touch with her real self at all; she is attractive to him because
she matches his image of what a delightful lady companion should be.
Like a frothy drink, their soirée is a pleasant way to spend time. But
it is still functional and all the more isolating because it skirts friendship, love and home.

In an age when we are free to be ourselves with complete honesty, why do we let ourselves look upon others in this pragmatic way
and call it friendship? The reason may be that the functional attitude,
for being intellectual and "data-based," is considered objective and,
therefore, the one valid way of grasping reality. In fact, an IBM ad-
vertisement said just that: "Not just data, but reality." John Macmurray would have replied: "Not reality, just data." He had exposed the
fiction behind the ad long ago: "This concentration on the object, this
indifference to the persons concerned, which is characteristic of the
'information' attitude, is often called objectivity. It is really only im-
personality."[2] The functional perspective is not in touch with the
other in his or her personal uniqueness at all. He or she has value to
me only in terms of my self-oriented need for the other for my use or
my delight.

But could there be a saving grace in a couple's delighting in one another's company and even in relieving one another's loneliness through sexual expression? The last half of the question traditionally invites a quick no; but could this not be a form of kindness to the other? Indeed, do we not pray to God mostly for help in our need or consolation in our sorrow and expect a kind Providence to attend to our yearnings? Maybe the last kindness a World War II pilot experienced in this life was the tenderness a British girl had shown him for those three months before his B-17 was shot out of the sky. The response depends upon how much sharing of personal truth had been kneaded into their relationship. Because without this sharing, there is very little sincerity behind the outward manifestations of care for the other. Only such sharing makes the relationship personal rather than merely functional. Functional associations are too concerned with self to allow for appreciation and gift to the other.

This was the desolating message of a play in the late 60s called *Moonchildren*. Three different couples had been "living together" in their final year of college. The drama transpires on the day after graduation when they break up housekeeping and say goodbye to each other with no future together nor really any past. In the case of each couple, neither knew the other's last name! So much for nonsharing— such fear of intimacy that the live-in lover knew less about his or her companion than the local department store. It wasn't so much that the bond did not take as that there never was any true conversation in which a person gives himself or herself away to a friend. Without such conversation, which is so much more than talk, sincerity lapses and the relationship becomes a sham.

Love, as Anne Lindbergh reminds us, is not based on the promise of duration; it is based on sincerity, appreciation and gift. Ironically, the Roman ethic that cast its shadow on American morality down through those same 60s insisted that the most essential ingredient in married love were the vows that endure. Is that what was really meant? Wasn't it rather that marriage had to endure since children were inevitably born to the union and had to be looked after in a permanent, stable context? And even if children did not come, the wife still needed the economic support of the husband so that divorce was out of the question. Perhaps the Roman Church's interpretation of Gospel statements about divorce reflected imperial policy insuring the common welfare rather than Jesus' concern for the individual person. (Or did Jesus talk annulment with the Samaritan woman?) Unbreakable marriage was indeed U.S. public policy until the post-war era. Two cultural factors changed all that: the contraceptive pill and equal opportunity for women in the marketplace. The pill became an effective method of birth control that allowed couples to express their love sexually without the prospect of pregnancy. At the same time, the opening out of job opportunities for women meant that they were no longer economically dependent upon a man in the house as breadwinner. Meanwhile, divorce had become legal in all the states of the Union. The ironic outcome of all this is that we now have a high divorce rate with a large percentage of our working women running households as single parents. This dramatizes how much public policy forbidding divorce may have hinged upon the inevitability of children being born into a marriage and the limited economic opportunities for women.

Before World War II, jobs for women were for the most part limited to teaching, nursing, and secretarial work, with telephone operators fitting that last slot. There were "normal schools" to train women as teachers and librarians, nursing schools, and secretarial schools. So, Lizzie's fear of becoming an "old maid" was not just in her head and for her to talk like a "schoolmarm" was an understandable "no-no" for all the Curry men. In the 30s, a good number of schoolmistresses were Miss for life; not to mention "Marian the librarian" of *The Music Man,* who was rescued from an uncertain future by none other than Robert Preston as Professor Harold Hill.

So we can't fault Noah on his law of averages. His shortcoming was in failing to see that Lizzie was not average, nor his brother Jimmy, nor Bill Starbuck. Like so many accountants that came after him, Noah was not venturesome. He was your hidebound institutional man: Plain girls don't get married. Item two: for Jimmy to be driving off with his girlfriend, Snookie, was inviting trouble—possible pregnancy and a necessary marriage. And for H.C. to let Lizzie spend the late night alone with Starbuck in the tackroom was madness, sheer madness. He'd be an uncle quicker than rain reached Kansas. Yep, Noah was your policeman—as inflexible as the Romans in his "protecting" Jimmy. Trouble was that Noah was a puritan, so much so that he intercepted Snookie's phone call for Jimmy. And like so many puritans, Noah had Jimmy looking forward to being with Snookie all the more because older brother had labeled her "fast." Since self-righteous Noah made Snookie out as "all bad," brother Jimmy considered her "Not bad!" Noah did have a way of making Jimmy feel wrong and under constant scrutiny. Noah was not all wrong in his attitude, just very one-sided and, therefore, prejudiced. H.C. could sympathize with his elder son because he had once been all work and policy himself: "Noah, when I was your age I had my nose pressed to the grindstone—just like you. Your mother used to say, 'Let up, Harry—stop and catch your breath.' Well, after she died I took her advice—on account of you three kids. And I turned around to enjoy my family."[3]

To enjoy his family: Taking a good look at each and loving each. Seeing the worth of each. Not binding any to efficient performance. Detecting the loneliness in deputy sheriff File. Seeing Starbuck's need to find his star, even if it meant raising the odds for thunder with a bass drum. This was Harry Curry, who harnessed his functional perspective when he left the grave of his beloved wife. The appreciation perspective that he embraced implicitly says: "*You are acceptable in your unique worth, just as you are!*"

Appreciation is not a matter of logic but of sincere interest. Logic cannot fathom the unique worth of another since it has no schema for uniqueness. Logic deals in categories, intellectually. But, to cite Saint Exupéry's most famous line, "A person can see clearly only with the heart; the essential is hidden from the eyes."[4] Noah's logic that pegged Lizzie as plain was factually accurate; but he was blocking out her personal side, her inner beauty. This would have meant giving way to the affection he felt for his sister, the way Jimmy did in his clumsy way. (Jimmy had tried to slug Noah for his devastating remarks to Lizzie.) Affection is not just a sign of appreciation; it is the only way of coming to know the inner beauty and unique worth of another person. For what is affection but my unique spirit *showing* appreciation for your unique worth for which there are no preset symbols. If logic becomes concrete in a word or number, appreciation becomes real only in some kind of expression: card, keepsake or roses. Without expression, a thought remains a wisp of an idea; without expression, appreciation is the stirring of a person's spirit that goes unacknowledged—to one's own loss and that of his or her friend, sister, brother, parent, spouse. As he did with so many dimensions in our living, the late Oscar Hammerstein II captured this truth for *The Sound of Music* in rhapsodizing that love is not really love until it gives itself away.

Because appreciation turns upon sensitive awareness of the unique worth of another that finds expression in affection, it goes counter to the Stoic maxim of keeping our feelings in check. Emotions are suspect for the Stoical mind and must not interfere with the efficient running of a farm or a household and "objective" assessment of a situation. That was the basis of Noah's functional perspective that could be so insensitive to Lizzie's feelings and to her worth as a person. He did love his sister but his Stoical side had numbed every other consideration. Emotions must not get in the way of efficiency or facing the facts! This was the way H.C. had run the farm until the day his wife died. That was the heart-rending experience that chased his functional priorities for good.

Harry Curry would never force anyone into a program. He would invite, but never exert pressure. Even in his concern for Lizzie's future, he could not again make the mistake of trying to set up a date for her with deputy sheriff File or with her cousins. All he could do was to respect others and offer them his trust, even if it went counter to logic. What he wished for every other person was the freedom to become himself or herself and not to miss what he had missed in letting his farm get in the way of "squandering time" upon his wife. He had his priorities straight now in full personal sincerity. Persons are more important than profits, than cattle, than the law, than local customs. Because of his appreciation attitude, H.C. could see the abiding hurt in the heart of File in keeping up the pretense that he was a widower. H.C. gently let him know that everyone knew his wife had run off with another man, and that their gestures of friendship to him were well meant.

This same appreciation perspective had Harry Curry take a chance on the rainmaker, Starbuck—who bargained to bring rain to the parched farmland for $100 and their full cooperation. H.C. instructed Noah to dole out the cash. This went against his accountant's grain so much that it pried Noah loose from the grip of his functional attitude. For the cooperation Starbuck required seemed as crazy as a jackass— and that was exactly what Starbuck asked Noah to do: to tie the hindlegs of the mule in the barn to shake down the heavens. Jimmy was to pound the drum and H.C. was to paint a line with metallic white paint to draw the portended lightning away from the house. About as logical as Ben Franklin hanging that key on the tail of a kite to draw electricity. But Noah went along with the illogic of it all because he knew why H.C. was doing it: not just for Starbuck but for Lizzie. To bring a fresh breeze into that careworn home. And Noah owed Lizzie; he had been wrong to be so factual with Lizzie; even he knew that people did not make marriage choices based on computer printouts. The mule kicked Noah. H.C. was flecked white. And Jimmy's drum brought File out to the house looking for Starbuck who was "wanted" for fraud.

But Starbuck had found Lizzie and was nowhere to be found when File inquired. H.C. covered as much for Lizzie as for Starbuck, with whom she was having the conversation of her life out in the tack-room. Noah's functional attitude had succumbed to H.C.'s prodding but not his puritanism—he wanted to go out and break up their "improper" get-together. Again, it was H.C. and his appreciation attitude that respected Lizzie and Starbuck's privacy by barring any interference from Noah. Meanwhile, Lizzie and Starbuck's appreciation for one another's unique worth had led to the communion of friendship.

Friendship is formed when the appreciation perspective blossoms into a truly *personal* attitude towards another person. The personal perspective implicitly says, *"You are beautiful and belovable as a person and deserve my gift."* The appreciation attitude discovers in you your inner beauty, your unique worth. But this "essential" in you, as Anne Lindbergh intimates, are your deep reserves for concern and care and total giving. Detecting this in you tells you that you are belovable as a person. Others can cook dinner and wait on table as well—but it is your loving way of waiting on table that reveals your personal side, if someone like Starbuck is there to get behind your shy, slightly aloof (for being hurt before) manner and take the risk of reaching you. In that risk is the initial gift.

Starbuck saw Lizzie's belovability as a person and risked rejection in letting her know that he found her beautiful. His gift was to invite her friendship. This is the first stage or moment in this personal attitude. Lizzie had responded positively by taking a pillow for Starbuck out to the tackroom. For this personal attitude cannot be one-sided: we have reached the realm of friendship which is mutual. Lizzie had let herself become vulnerable by letting down her reserve to reveal herself as interested enough in Starbuck to accept his invitation to personal conversation—that turning towards one another in listening care. In that conversation, Starbuck shares his dream and history of letdown with Liz. He reveals his vulnerable side, too. Friendship is a conversation, trustful communication with the sincerity that is not afraid to acknowledge weakness and admit to sentiment. (There's a world of difference between true sentiment that is appreciation issuing in affection and "phony" sentimentality that is "charm" with an ulterior motive.) Starbuck's verve is poetic, almost mystical—as he calls Lizzie "Melisande." He does this to have her break out of the factual pigeonhole where Noah has slotted her as plain Lizzie and acknowledge the mysterious beauty that is particular to each person. Starbuck once had himself been tagged as ne'er-do-well Smith: not the doctor or singer his older brothers were. But he had his star so he made that his name. He would "buck" for his star and never succumb to the "putdown" and self-righteous propriety of others. Their conversation has Lizzie literally let her hair down so that she could see herself as beautiful and beloved in Starbuck's eyes. She finds herself accepted for herself and loved for herself for the first time ever. Starbuck kisses her and in that moment she discovers the mystery of her beauty reflected in his sincere glance of love for her. She is ecstatic: "I can't *believe* what I see!"

But to invite friendship and then take off is shabby. A true friend stays with you after he or she has invited your trust and your self-revelation in friendship. This is the second moment in the personal perspective: readiness to stay with you in your response of friendship. This is crucial. For to raise another's hopes for friendship and then fade out is Don Juan-hollow and a violation of the sincerity that is the heart of love.

Yet it characterizes those who, like Philip Roth's Neil, mistake the pursuit of love for the belonging that is friendship. Psychologists suggest that this unstable notion can be engendered if one or other parent has become distant or unavailable time-wise and presence-wise during a child's formative years. If Dad never has time for his daughter because of work during the week and golf on the weekends, she resorts to all sorts of stratagems to win his affection. She is happy as a lark when he agrees to come hear her sing in the school musical on Sunday afternoon. He comes backstage with Mom while she still has her stage makeup on and kisses her (and her friends can see that her dad loves her). But then the interlude is over. It cost her so much effort to get him there, reminding him and hoping nothing would come up at the office at the last minute. Love for her has come to mean the search for her dad's presence and affection. She cannot trust that he is always present to her whether he's on the scene or not. Somehow he has not communicated to her his warmth and his concern and his "worship" for her that makes him present to her even if work or recreation call him away. (Children don't understand how much business is transacted on golf courses; maybe they're right not to.)

She has grown into an attractive girl as she enters college. But she doesn't quite believe anyone could love her enough to stay with her as friend. Her dad never seemed to want to take the time and rarely did—"It's the time that you have squandered upon your rose that makes your rose so special!"[5] She takes a liking to a certain boy in her English class and gets to know him in her unassuming way. She is guileless and refuses to resort to womanly wiles. He tumbles to her personal and physical attractiveness and asks her out on a date. She enjoys his company, he calls her every night, she dates him again and finds him a bore. This hunt is over. She needs to search for someone new since belonging is not meant for her. She doesn't trust that anyone could keep loving her in a way that would build a relationship. She doesn't feel that anyone would stay with her and keep being her friend. Behind her congeniality and attractiveness, she doesn't believe she is belovable because Dad didn't like to stay with her. If he did, he would have! So, love for her is the exhilaration of meeting new boyfriends and winning their attention and fondness for her—over and over again. She shuns those who get serious with her because, like Lizzie, she can't imagine anyone could keep loving her as she is in any permanent way. Anne Lindbergh's continuity in relationship that will deepen into marriage, family, and going through new doors is not meant to be hers. She does not believe in her inner goodness and sheer loveableness that would have any man devote a lifetime to her.

How much our high divorce rate has to do with so many of our young mistaking love for pursuit instead of belonging is difficult to say. But no child should have to win the love of a parent and "play games" to get him or her to stay. Nor should any friend or spouse. Starbuck stays; he asks Lizzie if he can. She runs into the kitchen and tells her dad (who is always present): "I've found me a beau." It is a beautiful turning point in her life.

If your goodness is what has me invite your friendship and stay with you as friend when your response is positive in my regard, that goodness deserves my total gift. This is not to say that our friendship will deepen to the level where we feel comfortable in making total gift to one another in marriage. But your goodness is worthy of total gift, and sincerity means that I am open to making such a commitment of myself. This is the third stage or moment in the personal perspective.

Goodness neither implies nor requires perfection in the other, as Thomas Butler Feeney's charming verse reminds us:

"Which is your favorite doll?" I asked
Of pretty Jane Marie.
"My old rag doll without any arms
I'm fondest of," said she.
"And which of these kittens that play about
Is the one you like the best?"
"Oh, the poor little thing without any ears
I love above the rest . . .
"And of all the boys I know at school,
The lad that I prefer
Is you!" she cried, and she skipped away
Before I could answer her.
So I looked at the blear-eyed cat she chose,
And the doll in faded pink;
Then I ran to the mirror and looked at me,
And I tell you it made me think![6]

Goodness means the quality in our friend that has her think of others and give of herself to others, even at cost to herself. Of course, we all have our mood swings. But this in no way overshadows our friend's goodness. Nor do we idealize that goodness because that would make her qualities a fiction. No, in her own quiet way she goes out to others in her special way of loving concern. This is her spirit, along with that shy little chuckle which is the signal that she would be embarrassed if someone made a fuss over her.

Starbuck is open to such a commitment as he invites Lizzie to come away with him. Lizzie has to make up her mind whether she wants to spend her whole life with him. For she now realizes there is someone else who wants her to be his wife: the deputy sheriff! File asks her not to go. She has always been fond of File, but this is the first time he ever talked marriage in his tongue-tied way. First time he showed any interest at all for that matter. File finally has enough emotional sincerity to speak his true feelings to Lizzie when it makes all the difference to her. He hadn't done so with his first wife and she had left him. Lizzie says Yes to File. Starbuck says, "So long, 'Beautiful,' to follow his star—as the heavens open up and weep rain for the joy of Lizzie. Also, for H.C.'s faith in the dreams of Starbuck, the faith that Unamuno extols as "trusting in life and abandoning ourselves to it, to life radiating from our own spirits, radiating from people and not ideas."[7] Yes, it was H.C.'s appreciation attitude that had let Starbuck be himself and Lizzie find "home" on his shoulder.

Though she did not choose Starbuck for her husband, he was the friend in whom she first discovered herself as beautiful and belovable. Because of Starbuck's friendship and sincere love for her, she could *believe* in File's proposal of marriage. Anne Lindbergh says that if we are stranger to ourselves, we will be stranger to others—and Lizzie at first acted as stranger to Starbuck because she was a stranger to herself. But Starbuck's open élan cut through her sagebrush of shyness so that she could believe in herself as deserving the lifetime gift of another. For if we do not believe in our own lovability as a person, no amount of attention and tenderness from another will do. This is probably why the girl whose father had no time for her blocked out belonging as her star. She did not believe in her belovability: it would take just a few dates for her newfound boyfriend to discover this, so she would have to settle for passing episodes of romance.

But what about Starbuck? If he really loved Lizzie, how could he stand by and take her rejection of him in favor of File? He had been true to the personal perspective in all of its dimensions and had ended up alone. The brief rejoinder is that Starbuck was sincere in his love for Lizzie. If I love someone, then it is her inner goodness and beauty, her unique spirit that engages my interest and care. What I want for her is her happiness, even more than spending a lifetime with her. She is no less good or beautiful because she chooses to marry another. It does mean, of course, that our friendship cannot take further root because her time and effort will now be devoted to her husband and family.

This is the great paradox hidden in the mine of human relationships: that the person who has overcome her diffidence and become herself in my trusting presence should go away to marry someone else. All we can say is that each person is a mystery because each person is unique. Psychologists help us understand why we make the choices we do, but in the end even they are baffled by the mystery of human uniqueness. Of course, I had hoped we would have shared a life together; but why she chose to dedicate her total capacity for gift to another rests in the unfathomableness of personal choice. Just as I cannot give a reason for my love for her—other than her unique spirit, so she cannot give a reason for her choice of another as spouse. There is no "how to" book nor quiz in the Sunday newspaper supplement to cover that. But we both had grown as persons in our gracious regard for one another since there was sharing in our mutual gift. Had we married, we would have married as friends, not just close acquaintances who spent good times together. Lizzie and Starbuck were friends because of their conversation in which they gave themselves away to each other. Lizzie supported Starbuck's dream and Starbuck had revealed Lizzie to herself as truly beautiful. Such gifts are blessings for a lifetime.

Starbuck and Lizzie discovered one another's interior worth because each had come to the appreciation perspective. Starbuck had reached it first precisely because he was not very accomplished by functional standards. He was thrown back onto the reservoirs of self-reliance where he tapped the springs of faith that Miguel Unamuno speaks of:

> Whoever has confidence in himself—in himself and not in his ideas—has faith in himself; whoever feels that his life flows, overflows from him, and carries him and leads him on, whoever believes that his life brings him ideas and that life takes them away also has faith.[8]

Starbuck was so in touch with the reality of the world through his vim that he never tucked anyone away in the concise file that logic provides. Lizzie had nearly been trapped into Noah's functional perspective until Starbuck came along and nudged her into looking out upon the world with the appreciation attitude. And she had found all herself in Starbuck's eyes. This description would seem to verge on sentimentality. Unless one has glimpsed the glow of a husband resting his eyes upon his bride of years going on yesterday. I have—beneath the star of their family Christmas tree. This is the knowledge that bears no explanation. Nor needs any.

The "star" of loving appreciation from another leads to the communion of friendship. Its light, as Saint Exupéry remarks, doesn't measure distance but reflects the presence of the beloved in one's eyes.[9] It can also be the star of Bethlehem in whose light one discovers the touch of God's love here on earth. This was the experience of Frances Farmer, a stunning movie actress of the late 30s, whose biography had given her every reason for her self-protective, functional attitude. She had been exploited terribly over the years on Broadway and in Hollywood. Her own mother, mistaking extreme hypertension for mental illness, had had her committed to an insane asylum. The ordeal she went through was almost too graphically portrayed by Jessica Lange in the movie, *Frances.* What the movie did not include were the later years of Frances in Indianapolis where she was hostess for a TV movie-program. She shared a house with a friend whose nieces had come over for a swim one summer's day. The children had just packed up and headed home, leaving Frances feeling quite alone in the backyard. She describes her great moment:

> Then I saw my "niece" Gina, who was twelve at the time, peek shyly around the corner of the house, and in the pure, simple voice of a child, she ran toward me, crying, "Aunt Frances, I didn't kiss you good-bye." I held out my arms to her and felt her nestle her cheek against mine, and in my ear . . . I heard, "I love you so much, because you're good." And then she was gone . . . As she left, a dry sob caught in my throat. No one had ever said that to me before. No one had probably ever thought it, for that matter; and it was there, at that moment, that a heart chiseled of stone melted. I could not hold back the floodgate of tears, not for being told that I was loved, or even good, but because my heart pounded with the joy and humility of belonging. On that quiet summer day I felt the first thunderous movement of God in my life, and

the soft voice of a child, the tender caress of her cheek against mine, had opened the door.[10]

The sense of belonging that Frances Farmer finally felt in the spontaneous love of Gina, Lizzie had found in Starbuck. It is in the mutuality of such moments that we experience the movement of God's love touching our spirits. This is blessing for both—the hint of the "eternal life" in belonging that Jesus spoke of to the Samaritan woman. The star of the Magi remains the brightest in one's personal galaxy because it leads homeward in the reassurance of being loved. No wonder Lizzie could say, "You look up at the sky and you cry for a star! You know you'll never get it! And then one night you look down—and there it is—shining in your hand."[11]

Starbuck's star was not so much in the rain that fell on the Curry farm that Kansas evening; it was in the glistening eyes of Lizzie who had received all his tenderness and gave him a sense of belonging for the first time in his wanderlust days. The functional perspective may catalog the stars as planets or asteroids. The appreciation attitude may see them as representing beautiful possibility in the human quest. But the personal perspective images in one star the presence of the beloved—the nearest star of all calling us home.

- 5 -

Distancing and Appreciation

THOMAS BUTLER FEENEY HAS A SIMPLE VERSE THAT DESCRIBES A MAN-
hattan apartment dweller taking his 8-year-old son on an overnight
campout in the Poconos of Pennsylvania. They are blessed with a
starlit evening as the father points out the Big Dipper, the Little Dipper, the Pleiades and Orion for his boy. Then comes the punchline of
the poem: "Dad, what in the name o' holy hell are they trying to ad-
vertise?"[1] Billboard lightbulbs were the only heaven the youngster
had ever known—so there had to be some practical purpose for all this
display. The father was stymied—the way St. Patrick's Cathedral is
by the buildings of New York City.

The pragmatic side of Manhattan is so preoccupied with the
value of real estate and advertising space that it crowds out other
points of view. The French don't go that route—they make sure
there's enough room around their great cathedrals so people can take
in their full beauty. They don't let skyscrapers put church spires in
shadow. (Nor do they turn their parks into parking lots; they keep the
autos underground where they end up anyway: even Ferraris turn to
rust.) Aesthetic symbols require vantage points to see them whole.
And the same holds true for recognizing the worth of a person. Anne
Lindbergh, when asked how to describe her late husband, spoke of
standing back a little and looking at his life in all its dimensions—like
a fallen oak. Appreciating beauty needs room for looking; appreciating the worth of a person needs distancing—something like the distance between actors and audience in a theater.

56

Drama critic Walter Kerr says the reason we go to plays is to step out of the swirl of everyday activity so that we can interpret our lives in and through the drama. He had difficulty, therefore, with the so-called "Living Theatre" whose presentation he had gone to review. At one point an attractive young actress had come right off the stage into the audience and given him a hug and a kiss. She had immersed him in the action of the play, thereby robbing it of any meaning for him. (His first reaction: "I don't believe we've been introduced.") And that's the way with life. We have to get away from the business of everyday to probe the hidden significance of our living in various aesthetic symbols like the theatre. But "Living Theatre" had dragooned the audience into its stage business, thus grounding the symbolism it may have wanted to put across. The actors had intruded upon the private space of the members of the audience so blatantly that it was no longer possible to discover any significance in the drama. It had become too "public"!

Drama is in a real sense a private conversation in which the actors convey the playwright's meaning to the individual members of the audience through word and gesture. Plays, like personal conversation, depend upon the active attention and imagination of the audience to interpret the meaning of the stage dialogue. The artistry of the playwright is in selecting words that are universal enough to appeal to a full house and yet particular enough to stir the personal reveries, the dreams and dreads of each member of the audience. Drama speaks to this private space in each individual and, like personal conversation, allows for pauses in the dialogue—for reflection. This is the distancing drama requires for an audience to comprehend its meaning. It is basically a private affair which bursts into shared applause because of its universal human significance.

Movies, however, are not conversational because the actors are not present communicating dramatic meaning to a particular audience. Films are pictorial, and with the advent of Technicolor, no longer concentrate on facial expressions and catchy repartee for their impact. Whether in color or black-and-white, movies are not "conversations" that depend upon the supple imagination of a listening audience to fill in the meanings prompted by the actors' lines. Movies are more like videotaped responses ("takes") of actors to their director which we are invited to play back afterwards. The director marshals all his expertise in visual, scenic and audial effect to blanket the screen with *his* interpretation of the actors' words and gestures. He supplies the meanings—leaving little to the movie audience's reservoir of remembered experience to put in the imagery suggested by the script. The creative imagination of the individual members of the audience has been engulfed by the director.

This is why we refer to films as the work of John Huston or John Ford—the directors. It is their vision of life as portrayed by actors like Robert Mitchum and Robert Preston and actresses like Deborah Kerr and Grace Kelly that leaves a lasting impression. But the players themselves cannot step forth from the celluloid and turn toward us. They are not speaking to us the way Richard Kiley did to me as a member of his London audience back in 1969. Our country was heavily involved in the Vietnam War that summer when Kiley was playing the lead in *The Man From LaMancha*. Late in that matinee performance, Kiley came on stage alone—his shoulders sagging, sat down on a platform, looked up toward us in the balcony and, with weariness lining his face and voice, whimsied, "If the whole world is insane, what is sanity?" He then stopped so we each could absorb the meaning for our time of that line of the supposed eccentric Don Quixote. We did not need an Associated Press Wirephoto to capture the overtones in Kiley's question; he counted on our own experience of our world flashing up the appropriate image. That fragment of a "conversation" never left me. Richard Kiley was looking right at me when he spoke and his gaze was still upon me in the silence that followed: I'm sure every member of that audience felt the same way.

But in making a film, there is no audience for the actors other than the director with his cameracrew and technicians. Even the actors are absent from the cuttingroom—so much so that Walter Kerr detects editor's fingerprints up and down the slots in the movie reels. (For the actors, the outcome is like the old poker game "Up and Down Broadway"—high risk that their best sequences will end up on the cuttingroom floor! Too bad it isn't Broadway, where at curtain time it's all up to the actors.) In this sense, the finished work of art is "public," like a painting that had no one in particular in view in its creation. Neither painter nor movie director can speak of a "live" house or a "dull" house the way theatre people do.

This may be what actor Lee Marvin meant when he gave his reason for not watching the movies he had made during his career. He found them to be "public." Marvin thought that what was most lasting in a lifetime were those mystical moments in which a man leaves himself and becomes at one with another person. There is no witness other than the person you shared it with—a woman, a child, another man. The late actor felt that, if you stacked those tender moments head to head and ended up with 27 minutes like that, you finished your life way ahead.

These moments of communion with those closest to our heart that Lee Marvin refers to presume appreciation for their unique worth. Such appreciation comes only in the distancing that is sensitive to the private space of each person. We may not force ourselves physically upon them in the "public" way of "Living Theatre." Nor may we impose our "idea" of how they must fit into our picture in the "public" way of a movie director or editor. Our friends are not our work of art. They are private persons who bless us with glimpses of their priceless worth if we don't saddle them with pressing attention or structure them into the scenario we image for them. This would be to disregard their uniqueness and treat them like all the rest—the public! This goes back to Harry Guntrip's insistence that we have enough trust in our own significance to wait upon the "time" of our friend's self-disclosure to us and not yield to the despair of physical clutching for her attention or of controlling her through the ideal image we thrust upon her. Only in distancing myself from my beloved enough to respect her private space and appreciate her unique worth can I close the distance between us and rejoice in the communion of friendship. Only then can she come all the way "home" and rest comfortably on my shoulder of complete welcome—just as she is.

All the Way Home is, in fact, the title Tad Mosel chose for his play about mending rifts in relationship by coming to full appreciation of another. Mary, a Catholic, prays to God for her husband, Jay, and herself: "Oh Lord, in Thy mercy . . . close this gulf between us. Make us one in Thee as we are in earthly wedlock."[2] Jay is not a churchgoer, nor a believer in the accepted sense. This bothers Mary and creates a gap in their marriage. The institutional Church comes between them, especially when their six-year-old son Rufus starts asking questions about the baby Mary is expecting. Jay begins to respond when Mary stops him. She informs Jay that the local priest said it was too early for sexual instruction. Jay is made to squirm for not fitting the role of father Mary's church has prescribed for him. He feels "superintended" by Mary in not measuring up to the image she envisages for him. Having given up alcohol for her sake and Rufus', he can't even make a little joke about the bottle without her getting edgy. Understandable for the heartache his former drinking had caused Mary; but it is another instance of his not being quite acceptable by Mary's standards. His wife has let her church dictate the idea of spouse and father Jay should be—with the local pastor acting as "director." This keeps Mary from fully appreciating Jay just as he is, in respecting his private space. Her husband doesn't quite match the "public" image of spouse and father laid down by the churchman.

It was Jay who created the distance that eventually narrowed to clear focus where Mary could see her husband in all his dimensions as a person. In the years of his wanderlust before settling down to steady work in town, Jay was on the road a lot. He would frequently stop at an all-night diner and drink coffee till sunup—conversing at times but alone with his thoughts. This was making more distance than even he wanted—"How far we come away from ourselves . . . Maybe that's where we're heading—to each other. And the sad thing all our lives is the distance between us."[3]

There is the distance that separates and there is the distancing that appreciates another completely. There was the distance caused by the institutional wedge between Mary and Jay within their own household. And there was the distancing that had Jay appreciating and missing his wife and child so much that he drove like the wind to get home to see them. "By suppertime tomorrow" had been his hope when the car crash happened. Symbolically, the accident that took Jay's life was at a bridge on a country road. Jay's death bridged the gap between himself and Mary that she had prayed about. There are few "shoulds" in our lives, but it should not have taken Jay's death for her to come to full appreciation of him.

Yet it happens so often that we don't embrace the precious worth of another completely until they are gone from us. When he or she is on the scene, we can yield to a tendency to refashion our beloved to our own specifications—which isn't love at all, is it? It may be that like Mary we have been conditioned into some sort of traditional image of what a friend or spouse is supposed to be and let slip the full blessing of his or her presence to us. It may be that we cling to the company of our beloved so intently that we practically force him or her to break free so as not to lose the distancing he or she needs to appreciate us! The great paradox in human relationship is that the dread of isolation that prompts the clinging to company makes isolation more likely.

Loneliness is the price of individuality since no one on this earth can possibly fathom the mystery that is myself, not even myself. When Genesis speaks of the effects of original sin, it is the absence of God from the garden of Eden that makes it no longer paradise. For only God as the source of our personal uniqueness beyond parental chromosomes knows each of us as we are. So man or woman is alone—though husband and wife do their best to close the distance between them, even if it takes a lifetime.

But there's all the difference in the world between a sense of loneliness and isolation. Loneliness is missing the company of the beloved but is a sure sign of the presence of the beloved "that blossoms a rose in the deeps of my heart"—to invoke a line from W.B. Yeats.[4] Loneliness may be inherent in my individuality, but in the company of the beloved I am palpably aware of the significance of my individuality. My unique worth rests in my spirit of gift, in my interest in and love for another person. My beloved in receiving this gift has reaffirmed my sense of personal significance. If home is her welcoming shoulder, her smiling eyes reassure me that she's glad for the gift of myself to her.

It is this image that keeps over the miles that may take me from her. My sadness comes in missing her company; but like a star she is ever present to me. I don't need the photo in my wallet to remind me of how she looks at me. St-Ex was right—the presence of a friend who is far away can be more real than physical presence. And that relieves the sense of isolation that might creep up on me. An old favorite song describes the home I shall return to where "two eyes of blue keep smiling through at me." There's the tip-off—I do have a home to return to in the beloved who is ever present to me. Saint Exupéry, who was too often an ocean away from those who were dear to him, captured this truth in a marvelous line: "Never were fiancés closer to their betrothed than when 16th-century Breton sailors were doubling Cape Horn."[5] That's the difference between loneliness and the dread of isolation. I am lonely because I miss the company of my beloved. But her constant presence banishes any sense of isolation. The distance becomes the distancing that has me appreciate her all the more.

The dread of isolation, however, casts in doubt whether there is anyone present near or far who cares to receive the gift of oneself and reaffirm a person's individual significance. Such desolation is a world apart from loneliness. For whatever reasons, this dread of isolation can overwhelm a person and obscure the presence of the beloved. The root of this despair may lie within the person himself where he doubts whether he is lovable just for himself. The functional world we live in, with its emphasis upon meeting a standard of achievement, can do that to a person. If the one we had looked to for appreciation and communion has unwittingly conditioned our relationship upon exacting performance and conformity to external norms, then we are indeed up against the spectre of isolation. In wondering whether we have a home at all to return to, we are worse off than the prodigal son.

When people come to doubt whether the person they love appreciates and loves them as they are, they deal with this anxiety in various ways. A man can bury himself in his work in order to "prove" himself—if he has the talent for it. Even if he doesn't become outstanding in his job, staying on the job long hours delays the feeling of disapproval that inevitably meets him on his doorstep. When a household has become an institution where one has to measure up and perform successfully, then the local tavern can become a haven. If the husband no longer shows appreciation for her, the wife will keep busy at household chores, neighborhood projects or take a job outside the home. Truthfully though, none of these engages a woman's capacity for total gift which Anne Lindbergh insists is peace for a woman. But a child can, especially if the husband has become distant. Still, for a husband to marry his work and a wife to marry her child in terms of time and total attention is a form of escape motivated by the dread of isolation. The job does give the man a sense of accomplishment; being a good mother does give the wife a sense of fulfillment. But neither pursuit yields the sense of full personal significance that once was affirmed by the beloved. The distance between has become a chasm which neither success at work nor the devotion of a child can bridge.

Both spouses have become defensive in the face of the studied aloof-ness of the other. Since each spouse still loves the other, each has to ask himself or herself what kind of censure he or she has put upon the other to make the spouse feel under scrutiny?

Two institutions come into play here that can put a person under judgment: the church and the family. Both preserve a pastiche of tra-ditions that the members of each institution are expected to follow. The irony is that the customs of a family were probably set down by a great-grandparent ages ago and the ecclesiastical norms by some Church Father or bearded elder centuries ago. What was a spontane-ous gesture for an ancestor has become rigid duty for the descendant. Many a college boy has been made to feel guilty because he missed the family Thanksgiving dinner to be with his girlfriend's folks in an-other city. ("All because a few Pilgrims missed Virginia and hit a rock! Thanks, I'll have mine 'on the rocks.'") And many a Protestant bride had to scrap her dreams for a wedding in her home church be-cause a Catholic boy had asked her hand in marriage.

Institutions have a way of flattening out personal space. When families become institutions where a spouse or a child is made to feel inadequate or not quite acceptable, escape is the only reprieve from the dread of isolation. The escape may be in miles or in alcohol or in drugs. Psychologists suggest that girls in their late teens who feel ex-tremely isolated within their family because of an aloof father and domineering mother often form sexual alliances as a way of winning personal approval from someone—at least for a time.

Such approval from family is what Jay's younger brother, Ralph, desperately sought in *All the Way Home*. The family had "institution-alized" Jay, looking up to him in a way that made his brother feel inadequate. (According to her biographers, Grace Kelly did not fit the athletic model her father admired in her older sister. Making any fam-ily member a model is a lapse that goes back to Adam's favoring Abel over Cain.) When we meet Ralph in the play, he is married with one child and is still trying to prove himself the equal of Jay. He takes out a loan so he can drive up in a better car than Jay's. He brags about his good credit rating, his funeral business, and the upbringing of his young son. But still, down deep he does not feel lovable just as he is. He is snarled in the functional perspective thrust upon him by the in-stitutional attitude of his parents. He is a stranger in his own family and a stranger even to himself, who can't appreciate that his wife, Sally, loves him for himself. He even accuses her of hankering after Jay; but this is just another manifestation of his feelings of inferiority. Ralph needs attention and reassurance of his worth so badly that he even hustles girls in the local movie theater.

So it is no surprise that Ralph resorts to a sure attention-getter—illness. Illness lays a claim on family honor to attend to a sick member. Ralph's sickness is his alcoholism. (British psychoanalyst, Ian Suttie, states that in many cases, alcoholism is a "flight to illness."[6]) Ralph's new car can pass anything but a gas station; Ralph himself can't pass a pub. Jay is the family member whom Ralph appeals to. Jay's having sworn off alcohol has made Ralph feel himself the black sheep in the family all the more. Ralph tugs at Jay's loyalty to family and sympathetic feeling for his brother in asking him to share the last swig in Ralph's bottle. With the other members waiting for them out at the car to start off for the reunion, Jay finishes off the fifth. Ralph has succeeded in bringing his brother back to his level in pressuring Jay to infringe upon his vow against getting drunk—a vow that Ralph could never keep.

If the institutional side of family had made Ralph feel inadequate as a person, fidelity to family was foremost in Jay's personal *credo*. There is this need at the heart of each of us to believe in something, someone greater than ourselves to give meaning to our lives. For those like Jay who reject organized religion, family often takes the place of God as the focus of their allegiance and loyalty. Ironically, it was Ralph's phone call late that same day that summoned Jay away from Mary and Rufus to attend to his stricken father. His goodbyes to his wife and sleeping son were to be his last.

But Jay didn't go away from home without leaving symbols of his presence. In one of the strange nudges of providence, he had just turned up an old plush dog he had given Rufus as an infant. And his last gesture as husband was to plump the pillow for Mary. He had told his wife its significance for him: as a child he had been afraid of being left alone in the cold of his bedroom, so his mother would plump a pillow and put it next to him to represent her presence. Little things mean a lot—and when Mary went upstairs alone after hearing the fading sounds of Jay's Ford marking out the miles to his father's house, Mary discovered the pillow meant to stay any chill of isolation she might experience. She could only exclaim: "Oh, the dear."

When the ambiguous call came next day saying that her husband had been in a serious accident, Mary needed the pillow of Jay's presence to cushion the blow. She had to come to grips with herself as questions about the accident flooded in upon her. Was he paralyzed? Had he been speeding? Had he been drinking? Was he dead? Then her brother Andrew returned with final word that Jay had died instantly.

From that moment, Mary shed every other consideration except that she loved her husband totally just as he was. Enough of the well-intended advice from her aunt about looking to God in bereavement— "You never had anything but God, Aunt Hannah. I had a husband. I was married to a man. I won't have God in his place."[7] Enough of having to apologize to Ralph for not employing his services for the funeral. Enough of her father's complaints about the priest's not blessing Jay's grave. Away with these "institutional" concerns: neither church nor family could bring Jay back. What she wanted now was a good drink.

Of course Mary was glad that both church and family stepped in to take care of the obsequies—the established traditions of both relieved Mary of an added burden. But within herself there was transpiring a conversion away from both institutions which had wrapped her in a constricted view of Jay. How she wished now that she had let her husband have the things that made him happy instead of harnessing him with "shoulds" about driving, drinking, and bringing up Rufus. As she walked away from his grave, Mary had let loose her functional attitude that was so keen on conformity. It had blurred full appreciation of that wonderful man who had come back from the Panama Canal Zone to make her his bride. She wished for him the complete freedom in being himself at the last: If he had been drinking, she hoped he had enjoyed it. If he had been speeding, it was because "he loved to go fast—racing to us because he loved us."[8]

Mary had finally gotten past institutional considerations and had taken on the appreciation attitude that let her see almost for the first time the profound worth of the man she had married. She felt full communion with Jay as she walked to the stairway window and looked out at the sky: "Be with us all you can, my darling, my dearest."[9]

Mary had said Yes to Jay's existence and worth as a person and, therefore, to her own. Jesuit Karl Rahner would insist that in such positive
affirmations about our existence we encounter God: "To accept and
assume one's human condition without reserve is to accept the Son of
Man because in him God has accepted and assumed humanity."[10]
Mary's prayer had been answered; she had come "all the way home."
The curtain falls with Mary telling Rufus about the baby in her womb,
picking up where she had interrupted Jay. She would now teach Rufus
in Jay's way. It would be easy because Jay had formed a bond with
Rufus that would keep beyond death. Rufus and Jay had "squandered
time" together, catching the same glimpse of the "North Pole" beyond
the Tennessee mountains.

The Manhattan man had done the same with his young son in
walking toward a Pocono mountain at dusk. And though the son saw
the heavens as "The Great White Way" instead of "The Milky Way,"
they were sharing an experience that would remain down the avenue
of years. Those trails in the Poconos trace the girlhood memories of a
close friend of mine riding horseback alongside her father. The skate-
scratches on a Long Island pond are etched in the memory of another
friend where, as a young mother, she shared thrills and spills with her
daughters. The experiences that weave the bond of relationship need
not be athletic; nor should they be too competitive for then they verge
on the functional and lose their unaccountable dimension. Anne
Lindbergh made sure that she made time to be alone with each of her
children, that way keeping any rivalry from intruding upon her appreciation for each.

It is only in such "useless" moments that you come to appreciate
the priceless worth of the friend, spouse, parent or child next to us. It
is the mutuality of such experiences that are transfigured into one of
those 27 moments of full communion with man, woman, or child that
Lee Marvin treasured. You never know when such a moment will
come to you. You may be walking around a park in the center of a
busy city—side by side with your beloved, not a word being said as
each of you respects the other's interior space. And of a sudden she
turns to you, her soft blue eyes all aglow for you, just you, as she puts
her arms around you, head upon your shoulder, and kisses you. That's
the touch of home, a starlit moment in midafternoon that keeps forever.

Or it could happen when we are taking in the beauty of a sunset or a hilltop vista with our best friend. We glance at each other in that instant and interiorly say, "You are priceless, too." Telling that to a friend solely in my glistening regard for her means "You are belovable always, you to whom I would make total gift if and when you are free to receive it." With a child, especially if the child is one's own young son or daughter, that time is always *now*, as it was for Jay and Rufus. Jay had prepared Rufus for his death in the mystery of those spontaneous sharings that are life's only real blessings. Relationships are a cluster of such experiences remembered in keepsakes, like Rufus' tattered plush dog.

For a former student named Eileen, the symbol of her bond with her dad is his beat-up baseball cap. They had had car trouble at dusk on a New Jersey parkway and had pulled over to the side to wait for a tow truck. A speeding car slammed into their car and her father died in Eileen's arms. One day she quietly told our class about her sense of her father's continuing presence to her. I asked whether she felt her dad was still proud of her when she did well in her studies. She said Yes. I asked her whether she felt he might be a little miffed with her if she messed up deliberately. She said Yes. I asked her whether he still loved her, no matter what. She said Yes. Finally, I put the key question, "Eileen what was it that formed the bond between you and your dad that makes him so present to you?" Her response was that they would simply spend time together on Sunday afternoons and play catch or go for a walk in the park. "It's the time that you have squandered upon your rose that makes your rose so special."[11] Eileen and her father had become friends as Jay and Rufus had.

It is so important to become friends—not pals exactly—but friends with our children. As my friend John Macmurray puts it in a line I never forgot, "Friendship needs no justification."[12] That was his resonance with Saint Exupéry. John was just saying, I don't have to be anyone but me and you don't have to be anyone but you, and what we choose to do, even share a life together in total love, needs no justification from anyone else." But sometimes it can happen that a person marries someone he or she really hasn't come to know in the unconditional way of friendship. Our dating customs may have something to do with it, where we try to keep our best foot forward so that the person we're so fond of will keep responding to our invitations to go out together. Now if we both start acting a part without having the complete honesty to disagree with the other for fear of losing the friendship, then there's insincerity at the heart of the relationship. Yet, we probably are not aware of it.

So when we marry, we must be sure we are marrying a friend. (Again, we don't *have to* from external propriety, but we *must* from interior sincerity.) And as Mary learned too late, we must not let any institutional consideration—career, politics, religion, "power" plays, finances, lifestyle—eclipse our vision of our beloved. He or she is simply too good to miss. Without his or her welcoming smile, our world goes dark. With it, not even death can erase our sense of significance in the eyes of our beloved.

- 6 -

Duty and Affection

MY DAD WAS A CIVIL ENGINEER FOR THE MEDUSA CEMENT COMPANY. As a boy I thought it a curious title because no one could have been more civil than my dad. He had grown up in West Medford, a suburb of Boston and had gone to college at nearby Tufts. But he was quite alone by then. His father had died when my dad was 15 and his brother was away in the Navy. There was just himself and his mom, who never quite got over the death of her daughter. Ellen had fallen from a swing in infancy. The solitude of his home life left my dad lots of time for reflection. Perhaps this is what nurtured respect for all other persons as the paramount value in his life. This respect showed itself in his good manners and treating every other as equal.

This is why when he arrived at the Dixon, Illinois plant with his Boston accent, my dad worked hard to flatten out the "r"s in his speech. In giving orders to the men under his foremanship, he did not want to come across as a Harvard professor. He was just plain Phil Mooney, engineering degree or not.

My dad was quiet and a good listener. There was either a lilt in his voice that signaled a quip or a reflective note that meant he was serious. Dad had to travel a lot for Medusa after his transfer to the head office in Cleveland, Ohio. He had become field engineer, which meant he was in Chicago, New York, Washington or York, PA every other week. The "overnight sleeper" to New York and "The Palmer House" in Chicago became part of our household vocabulary. He would get back from his trips Friday evening and go downtown to the office on Saturday and work till noon. So my chances of being with Dad were sparse.

I was in fourth grade then, and I recall one evening in summer his coming up our front walk after one of those trips and leaning over to kiss me. The gawky tomboy down the street teased me about it later. Maybe that's why I remember it to this day, because my dad broke out of his natural reserve to let me know how glad he was to see me and to be home. I also keep the memory of our last time alone together. I had saved up my money from work to take a trip East before going off to college. My dad was already there on business so we met in Boston. We took a walk along the Charles River where my dad used to row with his own father 30 years earlier. We had supper that night with his great-aunt Agnes. He mentioned afterwards how difficult it was for her to be "the last leaf on the tree" with all her family gone. My dad was in the grave three years later. But I was lucky enough to have had that special moment—the last strand knitting my bond with him. It wasn't the Poconos, but the evening star may have put its misty reflection on the Charles because we had walked till dark.

Father and son, father and daughter need these times alone together and breakthroughs of tenderness. With so many mothers now working outside the home, they too have to resist the relentless pull of the shopping mall to open up time for such sharings. The press of duty is a constant that cannot be allowed to prevent these chances. Our children go through our homes so quickly that we cannot pass up an opportunity too often or they will be gone from us. Your daughter is already 10, yet you remember the day she was born as clearly as yesterday! Double her present age and she's in college and maybe just a year or two from marriage.

We must create a sense of belonging with our spouses and children before it is too late! I'm getting a bit "musty" but those few years our children are under our roof are precious times in the full sense of that word: *pretiosa* for priceless. Our children cherish their private space, which we respect, but we cannot become so busy that we forget to show our feelings for them, especially when the blues of isolation come upon them. We ourselves had felt those aches as high school students trying to find our way on our own and needing to be accepted by our group. I used to think Jane Fonda was brassy and still feel her Hanoi broadcast to our troops was terribly insensitive. But when I found out later that her dad had forgotten her 16th birthday, I dropped my antagonistic feeling towards her. Her father had suffered greatly because of his first wife's infidelity; so we can feel for his insulating himself against hurt. But the cycle has to be broken at some point. His daughter was yearning for affection at a time when it was so important for her to have it: high school and her 16th birthday.

Breaking the cycle that blocks tenderness is the thrust behind Terrence Rattigan's subtly gripping play, *In Praise of Love.* On the surface the drama seems to be the typical British parrying with chit-chat. But churning beneath both spouses' repartee is the yearning for some sign of tenderness from the other. On Broadway, Rex Harrison played the lead as crotchety literary critic Sebastian Crutchfield. His wife Lydia, portrayed by Julie Harris, has been diagnosed as having an incurable disease that gives her only about six months to live. (Rattigan is said to have written the play for Rex Harrison whose wife, Kay Kendall, had succumbed to cancer at an early age.) Though Lydia screens the bad news from Sebastian by using her wartime-espionage expertise to doctor her medical reports, Sebastian gets the results on his own. Thinking she doesn't know the worst, he spends all his spare time and effort tracking down the best specialists in search of a cure. The prospect of losing his wife is devastating for Sebastian, but he keeps up the front of his usual nettlesome manner with her. If he started being nice and waiting on her, as he tells their friend Marc, that would rather give the game away.

The Crutchfields have a 20-year-old son named Joey. But there is little rapport between Joey and his father. Conscious of the short time she has to build some tie between father and son, Lydia gets Sebastian's commitment to be back at their apartment in time to watch the prize TV play Joey has written. Marc arrives; the show comes on and off before Sebastian turns up—too late. Sebastian takes Lydia's angry outburst, still refusing to tell either mother or son that he was delayed because of his appointment with a medical expert—his last hope for Lydia. He makes amends with his son in promising to watch a tape of the play with the TV critic on his newspaper, but not before adverting to the key truth in his past life. He tells Joey that, if his own father had acted that badly to him, he would have left the house forever. Joey thought he had done just that; but Sebastian corrects him in four desolating words, "No, I was turned out."[1]

Sebastian had never known "home" with his father. Nor had he in turn "squandered time" with either his wife or his son in a settled sense of belonging. Since being excluded from his own household, Sebastian had given up believing himself lovable as a person anyone would really want to share her heart with. So he hid in the haven of his work, for which he was quite talented. This is where he found his significance. But, in doing so, he had restricted his outlook on life to the functional: he did his duty as breadwinner for the household and did his job for the newspaper and did it very well. All this prevented him from forming any affectionate bond with his wife, not to mention his son. Consequently, he wasn't ready for the word that this would be his last year with her. The news of her impending death became the grace that dismantled Sebastian's witty facade and made him conscious of how much he really did love Lydia. The hatbox where he stashed his correspondence with the medical experts became the symbol for his pent-up devotion to her. This covert show of affection opened up in Sebastian the appreciation perspective enough for him to entertain the notion that Lydia might indeed love him. Up to that point, he had been locked into his protective strategems that also shielded any awareness of Lydia's affection for him. There is vulnerability in revealing one's feelings but more in receiving those of another.

Sebastian blamed his obtuseness upon the British taboo against tenderness, as did Lydia who sometimes wondered whether the British had any emotions at all. But there is more to it than that. Unfortunately, their first meeting at the end of the war was under the most functional and least personal of circumstances. Sebastian had taken advantage of Lydia's sexual services as an available woman he had met in the British bureau of occupied Berlin. Sebastian always had felt guilty about that, whereas Lydia had become attracted to him. He brings it up at the outset of the play and tries to abate his chagrin with another witticism. Sebastian is Marcel Marceau's clown who tries to conceal his sadness with a put-on chuckle, but his facial muscles pull the other way. In his own mind, Sebastian had "used" Lydia, an Estonian girl who had done heroic missions as an intelligence agent for the Allies. Sebastian felt it his duty to marry Lydia so that she could have a British passport to evade the Iron Curtain that had swallowed up her homeland. Lydia was delighted because she had fallen in love with

Sebastian and hoped to win his affection by being an indispensable housemate and efficient typist for his novels and criticism. Both Lydia and Sebastian were caught in the functional perspective where they thought each was acceptable to the other only for their usefulness. Because of the abiding hurt of being turned out of his house, Sebastian couldn't fathom the possibility that Lydia loved him for himself. In his eyes her dedication was gratitude for saving her from a bleak future in the Soviet block and earning enough to provide a comfortable household for themselves and Joey. She, in turn, had given up any expectation that Sebastian might come to love her and busied herself in making home life pleasant for him and being a good mother to Joey. She felt that Sebastian had come to depend upon her so much to take care of the details of housekeeping and his professional work that she kept her sad news from him. It reflected the flat state of their relationship that she would feel free to invite their mutual friend Marc to go off on holiday with her without Sebastian being taken aback. He didn't seem to care. Marc is the one Lydia turned to to share the truth that shadowed her existence. And it was Marc to whom Sebastian communicated his true feelings for Lydia.

It is significant that Englishman Harry Guntrip should have pinpointed the two ways in which people deal with their despair of ever forming a lasting personal relationship. We saw that one way was to seek the comfort of sexual involvement as the nearest a person could hope to get to another person. Sexual involvement before friendship forestalls rejection of oneself as a person. When the relationship falls apart, the given reason "After all, we hardly knew each other" actually infers "If she got to know me as a person, she couldn't possibly love me." This observation of Guntrip's fits Sebastian, especially in his uneasiness about having exploited Lydia sexually. Sebastian hadn't been on a serviceman's "Rest & Recreation" romp; he was dealing with the dread of isolation that his disclosure to Joey suggests.

Sebastian's incessant political arguments with Joey and his bookish discussions with Lydia and Marc recall Guntrip's remarkable insight that "if one has little capacity for having 'something in common' with other folk, then intellectual interests may give an illusory sense of still maintaining human contacts."[2] This description would fit Sebastian if witty patois and intellectual discourse were not his subterfuge to keep people from getting too close to him. He was not escaping human associations; he desperately needed them. But keeping his contact with wife and son at the discussion level warded off the possibility of Sebastian's being rejected as a person. "It is my outrageous ideas and ways of putting them that Lydia and Joey reject in me, not me" may have been the interior refrain Sebastian kept repeating to himself. He felt safe in his domain as a recognized literary savant until the stark medical report on his wife dented his armor and prompted him to be as honest about his feelings as he was in his opinions.

His most illuminating revelation about himself to Joey was his having been ostracized by his father. His most exhilarating while regretful revelation about himself to Marc was that he had always been in love with Lydia. It was the heavy crust of the British taboo against tenderness that had shielded this central reality about himself from his vision and had boxed him into his sterile functional outlook:

> I didn't really begin to love her until I knew I was losing her . . . Did I feel about her like this from the beginning? It's possible. And wouldn't allow myself to? Do you know what the English vice really is? . . . It is our refusal to admit to our emotions. We think they demean us. Well, I'm being punished now, all right, for a lifetime of vice.[3]

Continuing the cycle of repressed tenderness brought on by his unhappy boyhood had cost Sebastian. But as so often happens, the blowup brought on by his missing Joey's TV play, along with the drinks and *hors d'oeuvre's* that Lydia had so carefully set out, cleared the clutter that had jammed communication between father and son, husband and wife. In taking "both barrels," one from Lydia, the other from Joey, Sebastian stopped pretending to himself. Sebastian's significance did not lie in flaunting the Marxism of his youth in the face of Joey's interest in Liberal causes. Nor was it found in acting the part of "renowned critic," which he had thought was his only "drawing card" for Lydia. All his pretense had put him out of touch with wife and son. It was one thing to be preoccupied with trying to find a way of saving Lydia without her knowledge. But it was quite another to put upon his son the frigid impression of not caring that his own father had laid upon him.

Symbolically, it was the hatbox that turned the tide. Marc had suggested that the key to Lydia's happiness could be found there, and her discovery of all Sebastian's concealed concern beneath its lid brought Lydia to tears. So when Sebastian discusses with her how to write a note of apology to his son, Lydia, now rejoicing in her realization of his love for her, merely suggests, "Why don't you let him see you once as you are?"[4]

That's exactly what Sebastian does as he invites Joey to sit down for a game of chess before going to bed. Oh, he still hurls his Marxist epithets at Joey. But now they have no teeth but are terms of endearment, as Joey is quick to discern. (Our children almost instantly pick up when our "nasty" remarks have no cutting edge.) Sebastian had broken the isolating cycle in his heritage, that dreadful violence to family and friendship that put-down patter combined with stolid aloofness can inflict.

Sebastian and Joey are "squandering time" together as Lydia walks up to bed. At the turn in the stairway, she looks back at the two of them, her face all aglow because her longing for "home" between father and son is now being fulfilled. In the space of just a few minutes, she and Sebastian had shed their functional attitude towards one another in their wordless acknowledgment of how much each meant to the other. The hatbox was the symbol of their mutual appreciation: Lydia had forged the medical reports out of affection for Sebastian; Sebastian had sought all possible medical help out of devotion for Lydia. For her ears he mentions to Joey that the two of them might actually have a good time together while Lydia is away at a sunny resort. Sebastian then looks up from the chessboard to say, "Oh, sorry, darling, didn't see you were still there."[5] Lydia responds radiantly, "I know you didn't." She knows that she is never out of his sight and that her resort is in the communion between them now. (Marc had realized the revelation in the hatbox would keep her home!) Her glistening eyes evoke Saint Exupéry's line: "Eternal is the light in the eyes of your beloved when she smiles at you."[6] Sebastian would need that abiding image of Lydia's presence to face the darkness that would soon fall upon himself and Joey. As the curtain falls, he poignantly remarks to his son, "We haven't got all night, you know—Except I suppose we have."[7]

In his private conversation with Marc, Sebastian had been reduced to tears at the thought of losing Lydia. At that point, keeping a stiff upper lip made no sense, and Sebastian had had enough of the fiction about strong men not crying. If a friend loves a friend, if a husband loves his wife—that is deep sentiment which wells up in tears at the prospect of permanent separation from the beloved. Acknowledging our deepest emotions and the affection we really feel for someone lets us get on with our lives and our duties for the sake of our beloved.

Sebastian was on the mark in discrediting that taboo against tenderness which is another strain of the Stoic-Manichaean disparagement of the emotions. Repressing our true feelings is a dishonesty that casts a pall over our living as we reduce all our doing to duty. This closes down the appreciation perspective that alone leads to the communion of friendship. And without the appreciation and love of a friend giving significance to our living, we are thrown back on the defensive and feel, yes, feel we have to establish our significance on our own. We are fixed into the functional perspective as we become aggressive or manipulative in making others take notice of who we are. We have dug this trench in what becomes for us an uncaring world because we have repressed our emotional appreciation of the worth of the other. I see her only for my use and my delight. And if she becomes no longer useful or delightful, I drop her—never catching her glimpse of appreciation for me because the taboo against tenderness had disallowed such "sentimentality." British psychologist Ian Suttie verifies playwright Rattigan's insights into the harm caused by the trussing of tenderness:

> The repression of affection seems therefore to be a process likely to be cumulative from one generation to another. The mother who was herself love-starved and who, in consequence, is intolerant of tenderness, will be impatient of her own children's dependency, regressiveness and claims for love. Her suspicion and anxiety really amount to a feeling (rooted in self-distrust) that children are naturally bad and require to be "made" good by disapprobation and the checking of all indulgence of "babyishness." This creates a corresponding anxiety in the children about retaining approbation and winning more. The child feels too early that love must be deserved or earned, and excessive anxiety may easily reach the point of despair . . .

This may lead to a jealous competitiveness, the quest for power, position, "prestige," possession. Love has now become aggressive, anxious, covetous. Unintentionally, the mother has imparted her own inhibitions (or tender feeling) to her children, has substituted the ideal of duty for that of good fellowship and established a morality of guilt and distrust in place of that of benevolence and confidence which, I maintain, would have developed naturally.[8]

Interesting. How much of Sebastian's youthful involvement in the Marxist movement was a groping for significance that compensated for the lack of tenderness reassuring him of his personal worth. Antoine de Saint Exupéry anticipated both Guntrip and Suttie in noticing that people often take up causes to make up for the lack of a good relationship with those who mean most. To our dying day, we will seek personal significance. And if we despair of finding it in comfortable bonds with others, we may adopt a worthy cause—not even alluding to the fact that the cause is ourselves. This is not blameworthy because each one of us is a worthy cause. But how much political activism, for instance, camouflages a desperate feeling of isolation and a clawing for individual significance. We, of course, must be true to ourselves in following our convictions; and good arguments with family and friends about issues like war and nuclear power help clarify the issues. If, however, a person "protests too much," his or her interior motivation bears checking. For political argument can never salve the loneliness within. Only the affection and conversation of a friend can do that. How much political activism, for instance, has to do with a lack of fondness shown to young people, like Jane Fonda at an important time in her life. So it was more than love for Lydia that had Sebastian sit Joey down for a game of chess. In Joey, Sebastian had seen himself at 20 passing out political leaflets in lieu of the letter from home that would never come. Politics could never replace belonging. Duty could never cover a lack of affection. A hefty bank account could never make up the loss of not "squandering time" with those closest. The game could have been Monopoly or Scrabble. No matter. The intent was the same—"Just good to be with you!" Symbolically, Sebastian lost the first game quickly. We lose our independence to let someone we love get close to us—which is all we ever wanted. But, sometimes it takes us a lifetime to realize it.

- 7 -

Searching Significance

PERFORMING ARTISTS WORK BEFORE AN AUDIENCE. SO THEY TREASURE their privacy and inner space. Since playing a role—pretending—is their profession, they have to get clear of people to make clear the truth of their own identity. They need Anne Lindbergh's "Moonshell" time for interior reflection. Maybe this is why their words away from the spotlight often carry such wisdom. Grace Kelly, as a young actress, had to sort things out for herself in the face of the Hollywood power games of money and fanfare. Her inner clarity stayed with her as wife and mother in the palace of Monaco, where she was able to keep things in perspective. Shortly before the auto accident that took her life so young, she was asked how she would want to be remembered. Her response is Grace's signature of personal significance: "I would like to be remembered for trying to do my job well, for being understanding and kind, and as an honest person who cared for others."[1]

Princess Grace reflected that "truthfulness" which an opera singer friend of mine considers to be the mark of great performing artists. This friend has two daughters whom I have known since infancy. So it was no surprise that in the same newspaper interview their mother remarked, "If it comes to a choice between music and the girls, music loses!" She, like Grace of Monaco, had come to a settled sense of things; she has her truth. And it is reassuring in these career-engulfing times that a key part of the personal truth for both these busy ladies are their children. When her daughter, Stephanie, completed her *lycée* examinations, Princess Grace wrote a friend, "I'm finished school now." Mom's going over reading or arithmetic assignments is a memory the daughter cherishes more than being "belle of the ball," whether at a Monaco benefit or a New York school dance. Nose to nose over homework, parent and child walk the trestle of life together away from public notice. Doing numbers or words in the atmosphere of "home" is what counts and keeps with the child. Neither woman had let herself become sidetracked from the main truth about herself and the significance of her life.

In the totally sincere élan of their living, such women refuse to be distracted by those media pressures influencing our lifestyle that Herbert Marcuse alludes to: "The experts of the mass media transmit the required values; they offer the perfect training in efficiency, toughness, personality, dream, and romance. With this education the family can no longer compete."[2] Perhaps not the family in its institutional aspect, but the openhearted honesty of parents can—the truthfulness that doesn't waver before the wave of Madison Avenue advertising.

Audrey Hepburn suited Marcuse's description to a T (for Tiffany) as Holly Golightly in the movie, *Breakfast at Tiffany's*. She was very "mod" and the men came flocking to her. But she was still searching for significance in her living. She, like so many in their 20s, hadn't got straight that commitment to another person who is totally devoted to her is not a bridling of freedom but its fulfillment. Each of us is lovable and designed for giving. The choice of freedom is to whom to give my heart and my living. Not to do so is to keep bumping into myself in a boring way each day, only to ask myself: "What's up?" My life is—until I settle the truth about myself that yes, I do have interior worth, and that the friend recognizing that worth is not after shackling my aspirations but would set them free in his or her loving regard. This is what Paul, the one non-"gallant" companion of Holly's, (played by George Peppard) puts across to Lulu Mae—Holly's honest name:

> You know what's wrong with you, Miss Whoever-you-are? You're chicken! You've got no guts. You're afraid to stick out your chin and say, "O.K., life's a fact. People do fall in love. People do belong to each other because that's the only chance anybody's got for real happiness. You call yourself a free spirit, a wild thing, and you're terrified somebody's going to stick you in a cage. Well, baby, you're already in that cage; you built it yourself; and it's not bounded on the west

by Tulip, Texas nor on the east by Somaliland. It's wherever you go because wherever you run, you just end up running into yourself.

Lulu Mae got a taste of truth from Paul and, thanks to him, found her own.

But at least Lulu Mae had stayed with the quest. As we meet Carl Hofstra, played by Robert Mitchum, in the film, *Reunion at Fairboro,* he has stumbled into himself once too often and is about to pack it in permanently. Sixty, Hofstra has just been forcibly retired by his conglomerate after serving as CEO for one of its divisions. Good severance pay, plush apartment on Chicago's Lake Shore Drive, two divorces, no children fill out his current status that yields no personal significance for Carl. The lines are drawn long in his face as he finishes his can of beer, takes out the revolver from the drawer of his bedside table, listens for the bullet in the barrel—but some unfinished truth from his past makes him hesitate. He puts the gun away just as the phone rings from the lobby downstairs. It's an old Air Force companion from World War II, Nate Barsky, who invites Carl to the reunion of their squadron. Carl at first begs off—the reunion is to be in England—but he cannot refuse Nate's request to bring Jiggs Queeley. Jiggs is a down-and-out alcoholic now, but he had saved one of Carl's crew when their B-17 had landed in flames. Carl takes on the responsibility of Jiggs and recovers the truth about himself.

Sitting with Jiggs on the train from London to Fairboro (Farnborough) with shady countryside rolling by the windows, Carl's memory jumps back 40 years to 1944 and riding bicycle near his airbase with Sally Grant. (Here is what movies as an art form do best: in their flashbacks they present the memory image. This is marvelously done in *Reunion at Fairboro*, where the current action is shown in color while the flashback is filmed in the black and white of World War II.) Sally is the key to his past. So he takes a stroll from the hotel in town out to the small cottage he had once known so well. A 19-year-old girl is cleaning the yard. Carl almost shyly asks if a Sally Grant still lives there. The girl informs Carl that her grandmother is minding her boutique in town but that she would give him a lift there. The conversation into town is sprightly because the girl, Sheila is her name, immediately confronts Carl about being one of those American veterans come to town to booze it up and relive wartime exploits. She is critical of such gatherings because in her mind they glorify war and, besides, she is actually going into town to work on the anti-nuclear missile demonstration coming up in two days. Whew! Carl hears flak whizzing by his ears, but out of respect for Sally he doesn't argue. Sheila then tones down and asks whether he had known her grandmother during the war? Carl responds pensively that they had been friends but that she probably wouldn't remember him—so much had Carl's self-doubt clouded his confidence in Sally. Sally is in the back when Sheila and Carl enter the shop, so Sheila raises her voice to say she has brought an old friend. Sally comes through the draped doorway and is stunned to see Carl, who can only say, "I guess this was a dirty trick." Sheila sees the knowing look on her grandmother's face and asks, "Is that him?" Sally, still in shock, just nods her head Yes, whereupon Sheila looks up to Carl and gives him the zesty greeting, "Hello, Grandpop." It's Carl's turn to reel. His unfinished truth has circled back upon him.

He and Sally had not been casual acquaintances. They were very much in love and she had been his support and solace as he risked his life daily, piloting his B-17 over Germany. Sheila would later question her grandmother in private about the relationship and Sally, portrayed by Deborah Kerr, reassures her granddaughter that she and Carl were serious in their love for one another. Sheila sparks back, "But you were only 17!" Sally speaks for all of us who were 17 then: "You grow up fast during a war."

Few statistics from World War II are as startling as those of the heavy bombers of the U.S. Army Air Force flying sorties from England over Germany. From January to June 1944, out of every 1000 pilots and crewmen manning those aircraft, 738 were killed or missing. (This is not to mention those wounded.) So, every time an airman climbed aboard his B-17, he realized he had less than a one-in-three chance of getting back alive. The B-17's were very slow and their fighter escort could only accompany them as far as the German border before turning back for lack of fuel. The heavy bombers were sitting ducks for the very accurate German ack-ack guns.

One of the beautiful scenes in the movie is of the memorial chapel at the military cemetery near Cambridge. The chancel is starred with brass crosses, and the legend across the top of the grillwork reads, "Lord, into Thy hands I commend my spirit." Those young men were going out to their deaths with courage and spirit because of their loved ones back home. In the movie, Carl's beloved was Sally Grant. Carl and Sally fill in the gaps of their history over dinner that evening. Carl had not known that Sally was carrying their child when he was transferred back to the States in early 1945. Sally had not told Carl she was pregnant because she did not want to burden his life. Their daughter was named Susan, who died with her husband in a motorcycle accident at the age of 23. Modestly she tells Carl that Susan had Carl's good looks and not so modestly that she was as headstrong as he. Just as Sally had taken full responsibility to raise Susan by herself, she did the same for granddaughter Sheila. When Carl presses Sally with his right to have known about his daughter, Sally puts it right back to him, "What would you have done? See, even now, you're not sure." Carl's silence would seem to confirm Sally's point, except for his own history between. His first wife wasn't able to conceive a child, much as they tried; eventually they grew apart and divorced. Carl then married a divorcée with two children of her own. She refused to have another, depriving Carl once again of the chance for family. Their marriage broke up too, leaving Carl with business success, financial prosperity and an empty life until Nate came along with his invitation.

Strange how our lives unravel and entwine. Perhaps the underlying reason why Carl's two marriages didn't work was that his deeper bond was with Sally, and that neither of his two succeeding mates could ever take her place. At the reunion he meets George, another old crew member, who is an Iowa farmer now. He is not doing so well financially, but George is quite happy with his wife and six children who help him with his work. This contrast with his own life wells up in Carl and at the dinner-dance he attends with Sally, he blurts in her ear, "I had it all but I blew it." Carl had a family in the making but he had shipped out and never got in touch with Sally again. Sally tells him to stop tormenting himself. Carl is not very happy with himself at that instant anyway because of the blowup he had that afternoon with his granddaughter, Sheila.

The three had met Nate Barsky to go to the cemetery together. Sheila had been at Carl's shoulder when tears came to his eyes at the name of Ken Donegan inscribed on the monument. He had wanted to meet Ken again. Ken was his best friend. But the day Carl left England, he had slugged Ken instead of saying goodbye because Ken had asked about his relationship with Sally in a rather vulgar way. Carl had been so sensitive about his love for Sally that he failed to realize that Ken couldn't have known how serious Carl was about her. One of life's lessons is not to be put off by the brusque manner or seemingly crass words coming from a friend. Communication between friends is not a press conference with the diplomatic corps. What seem like Anglo-Saxon crudities not to be spoken in polite company can be the clearest kind of communication between friends. Refined language can mask utter cruelty: Elizabeth of England was quite well spoken when she asked for the head of Mary, Queen of Scots. But straightout language can come from the heart which a true friend can accept without wincing. We each would hope our best friends would speak in whatever way they want to in our presence. But, Carl had been all mixed up about leaving Sally when Ken had made the remark, and all his frustration had found its mark on his best friend's chin. Carl never saw Ken again. His granddaughter was right with him as he made his peace with Ken. The two pilots had gone through too much together not to be friends still. Their bond stayed intact though death and 40 years had intervened. Sheila had said it all, "If you can't weep for him, who can you weep for?"

Sheila drops Sally off at the shop and drives Carl back to the cottage with her. But they are hardly out of the car when Sheila aims another of her slogans at Carl, "I think all this talk of planes and missiles is insane." Carl has had it—so he fires back, "You don't think at all, kid. If you had a fresh idea, you wouldn't know what to do with it. You're full of crap." Sheila blanches at the blow, turns and goes inside. Carl, honest but also regretting his outburst, closes the gate and walks back to town alone. On the dance floor that evening, Sally reassures Carl with just two words, "She's young!" Never having raised a child, Carl didn't realize that it is misdirected concern to ride the moods of our children who are trying to find themselves in their late teens and early 20s. Such a waste of psychic energy! The anxiety that a 23-year-old tells you about on a Monday has disappeared by Wednesday, so it helps not at all for a parent to still be worried about it Friday. Our children in their 20s going on 16 just want us to be "on call"; but such "emergency" duty is best served by closing the book on yesterday's crisis. That's the wisdom Sally's brief comment carries for Carl. But Carl is desperate to find significance in his living, and Sheila had brought him a glimmer of hope.

But half a truth is sometimes more than half a lie, especially when it has to do with ourselves. It was safer for Carl to talk to Sally about his building a relationship with his granddaughter than to face his deeper truth. What Carl really was yearning for was full reunion with Sally in marriage. But fear of rejection obscured this for Carl, even though Sally has given him no sign that she would turn him down. In exchanging their histories earlier, Sally had made it clear that she had never seriously considered marriage with anyone else after Susan was born. But, Carl was sincere and sensitive in not trying to close the gap of 40 years with empty talk. He needed to probe the sense of things and fathom Sally's feelings. She had thought the dinner dance would be the happy culmination of their reunion. But Carl prevailed upon Sally to spend the night together in a Cambridge hotel after the dance. Perhaps it was the appropriateness of this for this couple who had never really stopped loving each other over four decades that clarified their relationship for Carl—and for Sally. (In our permissive times, sexual expression often occurs without mutual personal love; this reunion of Sheila's grandparents in total respect for one another as person is an instance of sexual expression of love outside of marriage that is very moral.)

The movie portrayal emphasizes the conversational dimension of the intimacy between Carl and Sally. Carl tells Sally that he wants to stay and be with his granddaughter as she reaches adulthood. Sally is very direct with Carl, "Sheila's all right and my life is in order. The problem is with yourself." Carl replies, "I'm not trying to change your life." Sally's response puts everything in focus: "I wanted to say the same thing to you 40 years ago." If a friend tells you that she is not trying to change your life, she really means that she is ready to adjust her own to build a lasting bond with you. But you were about to express the same to her—meaning that you would rework your life for her sake.

Growth in any relationship depends upon the willingness of both friends to alter their lives out of love for the other. But, for whatever reasons, Carl had never come to the sense of self-worth that would have him believe that someone was willing to repattern her life for him. His description had hinted that in his two marriages, Carl had accommodated himself to the wishes of his wife as the condition of the bond. Carl may have gone along with this one-sided insistence of his spouse so as not to lose her companionship. But his marriages were partnerships that fell short of the union of friendship. True friends affirm the beloved totally and are ready to refashion their lives for their best friend. This is why marriage can only work if a person marries a friend.

If one friend sets all the conditions in a relationship, it cannot last because that supposed friend does not fully respect the worth of the other and in a real sense does not love him or her. A friend shares everything with the beloved, including the weaknesses that they don't reveal to outsiders. This is why the heart of friendship is reaffirming the worth of the friend as the basis for one's love for him or her. When one friend no longer respects that worth and sets up hedges in the relationship, the other has to break off sooner or later. Full mutuality has subsided and one's search for significance cannot put up with such trampling indefinitely. It is mistaken devotion that attempts to sustain a relationship when the beloved—and she may still be the love of his life—disdains it. But now Carl, perhaps for the first time in his life, has come to realize that there is someone whom he loves who has never undercut his sense of worth and lovability as a person. Sally has been the "star" leading Carl to his truth, even in assuring him that she will keep their reunion as a beautiful memory.

Carl's squadron is scheduled to leave on the morrow. So next morning he stops in at the anti-nuclear rally headquarters to see Sheila. The place is hopping with last-minute activity because the protest at the Greenwood Commons is to begin that very afternoon. Carl tells Sheila that he's sorry for having popped off and that he has just come to say goodbye. Sheila is still in a huff and won't give him the time of day. That does it: Carl gets up on a table and confronts the group. He tells them to take a good look at him and asks if they think he wants to blow up the world. He turns towards Sheila and says, "She does." Carl goes on to say that there are as many Americans opposing nuclear warheads as English people, that he thinks nuclear missiles at the ready may actually be keeping peace but that he's not claiming to be right. He asks the group not to take everything they don't like and lump it together and call it American. He finishes by saying, "If you know me and don't like me, that's fair enough. But if you don't know me and still don't like me, that's damned nonsense." The older woman in charge asks Carl to come down from the table and have a cup of tea. But, Sheila, bursting with pride at the sheer courage and honesty of her grandfather, gets her things and accompanies Carl out the door remarking, "I think you need somebody to look after you."

They take a drive out into the country in Sheila's car. She tells him that she didn't really mind being an orphan until the other kids in school found out. Carl says that he had zero to do with who she is but Sheila reminds him that he is her own flesh and blood. They get out of the car to take in the hilltop vista, just as a British Mirage jet-fighter swishes overhead. This prompts Sheila to ask her granddad whether he can still fly. Carl answers that he doesn't know because he hasn't piloted a plane since he left the service. Sheila exclaims that if she could fly, she'd love just to get up and away to experience a complete sense of freedom. This conjures up all sorts of images for Carl, who had been the best pilot in his squadron.

On the runway of the airfield, Carl had seen his favorite plane, the AT-6. For the memorial service at the cemetery the day before, the plane had done a flyover during taps for all those men who, as Nate Barsky put it, "so long ago, so reluctantly laid down their young lives." Sheila's words work their way into Carl's spirit. He asks her to drop him off at the airfield on her way back to town. Carl climbs into the cockpit of the AT-6 and looks over the controls. All his know-how comes back to him as he revs the engine, checks the propeller pitch, speeds down the runway and puts the plane in the air. He flies over Sally's cottage and buzzes it; she comes outside and Carl wing-waves at her his second time around. Sally grabs her coat and heads for the airfield. By this time Sheila has linked arms with the other protestors at the Greenwood Commons. The AT-6 comes in low and does a passover that catches Sheila's attention. Carl circles and comes back along the line of protest and does a wing-wave for Sheila's bene-fit. She recognizes the plane and yells, "It's my grandfather." By this time Carl has attracted the notice of the air patrol who signal for him to land. The old AT-6 comes rolling up to the gate just as Sally ar-rives. As Carl climbs out of the plane, raincoat and all, the police approach him and ask him to come to the station. But not before Sally comes up and kisses Carl and tells him that she'll have tea ready when he gets "home."

Risking embarrassment had been harder for Carl than putting his life on the line during all the missions he had flown in service. He risked making himself a fool at the protest headquarters and had won over his granddaughter. He risked arrest in following up Sheila's nudge to fly again and he did it just to let Sally know how much he wanted to remain with her and Sheila.

Flamboyant and found only in movies? I don't think so. No more than for Lt. Henry Coakley when, early in the war, he buzzed his wife's home in Cleveland, Ohio. This became her last memory of Hank because his plane developed a problem an hour later and crashed near Wright Field in Dayton. (There are so few moving parts in a jet-engine that we have forgotten the many plane crashes caused by piston-engine breakdowns.) Hank's was the first and only serviceman's funeral I attended. So few of our servicemen and women have died on American soil that since World War II I've been quite hesitant about U.S. involvement in foreign wars. I was the youngest member of our football team that played in Coakley's backyard; Cliff Duffner was one of the older players. Cliff survived the war, but because he had made a mistake on his discharge papers, he was called back for the Korean conflict, where he died. The French found it a short trip to place flowers on the graves of their fallen, as did the Germans. But it was very hard for their U.S. families to get to the Bas-Rhin to visit the graves of the 7000 American soldiers who died to save Alsace, not to mention Normandy and Belgium. No, at least Beth Coakley could visit her father's grave at Calvary cemetery in Cleveland, Ohio. And I'm glad her dad had the good nonsense to buzz her house because she and her mother were the only reason Hank had gone to war in the first place. In the movie, Sally was the only reason that made chancing his life worthwhile for Carl.

Men like Hank Coakley and Carl Hofstra were as pacifist as Sheila's group. What seemed like the militarism of these two Army Air Force pilots, one factual, the other fictional, was really their protective arms wrapped around those dear to their hearts to save them from the atrocities visited upon so many European families during the war. Even in our own time, certain pacifists charge President Reagan with the tired cliché about his being a quick-triggered militarist, yet were silent at his signing of the anti-nuclear missile accord with Secretary Gorbachev. His confidants suggest that what made President Reagan approve the arms-for-hostages negotiation in the "Irangate" affair was his compassion for the relatives of those in captivity. Some pacifists are quite aggressive and some militarists cannot stand to see any family suffer. Labels in these matters can be very misleading. John Macmurray was a Quaker who felt it went against the spirit of peace to use pacifism as a demonstration of power. For him, all show of power crystallizes opposition, which creates division rather than peaceful community.[3] Antoine de Saint Exupéry would add that supporters of a cause like Sheila's antinuclear movement are actually searching significance.[4] Perhaps that is why Sheila was so quick to drop her work for the protest once she realized how much Carl Hofstra meant in her life.

It is ironic that, in rendering himself totally vulnerable to the antipathy of Sheila's office group, Carl had gotten through to his granddaughter. All he was asking of her was to be truthful and not to hide behind a protest sign in searching out her own significance. Sheila did go ahead to her demonstration later, but no longer out of any need to validate her personal worth. She had proudly walked out of her headquarters, her arm on the shoulder of a 60-year-old man who loved her more than anyone else on this planet. No, she could no longer characterize Carl as a representative of an "institution" that was endangering this planet. He was a man 40 years her senior who was younger than springtime for her because he wasn't stodgy and stuck in his ways. And he listened; in fact, he hung onto her every word so much that Sheila at times couldn't even look in his eyes. She couldn't have known how precious the moments with her had become for Carl. He was always ready to walk through new doors with her and for her and yet would never crowd her space. He did not, as some parents do, make her feel guilty about participating in the protest movement whose goals he did not agree with. He did not pull her off the line of protest or make any wisecracks about it. He respected her differences from him and her own special worth as a person. And above all he did not put her under judgment, much as he might disagree with her at times: his exasperation with her was in not doing her own thinking but echoing somebody else's party line! Carl was interested in what Sheila felt and thought—not in what her companions found acceptable. Carl's need had been to get Sheila off on her own as his one last chance for a good conversation with her: two's a couple, three's a crowd! But it was Sheila who, in walking out the office door to "look after" Carl, was smiling in the company of the friend who would always "watch over" her. No wonder she wanted to "hang out" with Carl and squander time upon him. When she saw the lines of concern creasing his face, she realized that those were the mapping of 40 years of his own search for significance in finding home with her and her grandmother. When she called out to her companions at the Greenwood Commons that it was her grandfather waving at her from the sky, *she* was exulting in having found home with him.

Her grandmother had thought that Carl would be gone with his air group back to the U.S.; but Sheila knew otherwise. She realized that in letting him off at the airfield, he was about to fly the sky where he and Sheila could together search the stars at night. It was his home sky now, and beneath what she had first thought to be the crusty facade of her old war veteran of a grandparent was a friend growing young in her presence. Carl hadn't smiled until he had climbed into the AT-6 and flown over the places where his beloved would be listening and awaiting his return. The clutter of 40 years of regret and inner anxiety was jettisoned in that single flight. He knew that when he landed, he would be surrounded by the affectionate, welcoming smiles of Sally and Sheila. Carl was home at last.

Searching significance means cracking the categories. Discovering one's own truth and finding home with the beloved means saying Yes to one's own existence and saying Yes to the worth of every other person, however much a failure he or she may seem in the institutional eyes of society. Perhaps the key to Carl's finally being able to say Yes to his own questioning of his personal worth was in affirming the worth of Jiggs Queely. Carl's support had put Jiggs on the road to personal rehabilitation; but Carl would have been there to help even if Jiggs would have "fallen off the wagon" and gotten drunk again. Our personal reinforcement of the morale of someone with a drinking problem goes beyond the U.S. puritanism whose chill disapprobation compounds his or her sense of failure. Ronald Reagan's own father, Jack, was burdened with this affliction. But, as the President himself told it, his mother confided in her boys that their father was not to be loved the less for his problem but needed their love and support all the more. This was Protestant Nell Reagan speaking on behalf of her Irish

Catholic husband. No puritan, Nell, but a true follower of Jesus who got beyond institutional categories to the person. With Nell's and the boys' encouragement, Jack Reagan was able to keep on top of things. He never failed to appear each morning in shirt and tie, ready for a day's work at the Pitney shoe store in Dixon, Illinois.

It was this same Nell who invited the black orphan boy, Winston McKinney, to dinner at the Reagan home so often that he would later refer to Nell as his foster mother. This lesson of Nell's left its mark on her president son, who never invoked his boyhood friendship with Winston to defend himself against the attacks he endured from various black organizations. For the president, these were further instances of institutional disapprobation that his own father had suffered! Sports announcer that he had been, Ronald Reagan may have taken his cue from basketball player Bill Russell who, when asked upon his retirement whether he would join a "black power" organization, responded, "No, I don't need that; I know who I am." Institutions have a way of getting in the way of our sense of our own worth and our regard for other persons, and Bill Russell would have none of it.

Bill Russell was in his own way reflecting his Jesuit education at the University of San Francisco. At the heart of this vision is the priceless worth of each person, no matter how formidable the institution that would put someone under judgment. In the Jesuit perspective, it is God our Father, as revealed in Jesus, who vindicates our personal worth that no institution may displace. The same Jesuit Karl Rahner, who insists that we encounter God in afffirming the existence of our neighbor, portrays those imbued with the Jesuit spirit as "people who tend to take everything in a relative manner apart from God alone, who is beyond reach and cannot be manipulated by humans." Rahner's full description disperses all the institutional "fallout" that could cloud our perception of what is really important in our living:

> People of this stamp cannot identify themselves in an absolute manner with any given time or with its attitudes, culture and systems of knowledge. Such a spirituality may occasionally give rise to compromise or to oversimplification, but the underlying attitude is deep, genuine and original. God is always greater than culture, than science, than the Church, the Pope, and all forms of institutions; none of these can substitute for Him. That is why a Jesuit always casts a critical eye on his

own past, even when it is touched with glory. And he remains open to everything new precisely because he cannot absolutize anything.[5]

What is the newest feature about each person is his or her possibilities for the future. Jesus himself had little truck with those who would block those opportunities for a bright tomorrow with their wooden judgmental outlook: "Why do you bother with the splinter you detect in your neighbor's eye when your own outlook is impaired with a two-by-four?" (Mt. 7:2) If there is one refrain that comes through loud and clear in the life and teaching of Jesus, it is God the Father's refusal to let past failures encumber the future of any of his sons or daughters. If Magdalene's past was shadowed with prostitution, Jesus, speaking for the Father, sets aside her condemnation in the institutional outlook of Simon the Pharisee with his strongest endorsement: "Her many sins are forgiven her because she loved much." (Luke 7:47) Sad to say, not even divine forgiveness is enough to dislodge the inexorable judgment of society. Giuseppe Verdi, in his opera, *La Traviata,* has the former courtesan Violetta give voice to this despondency in a poignant musical line, "Even if God forgives, humans remain implacable."

For many of us, coming to the personal truth that we are lovable just as we are—enough that a person like Carl's Sally or Holly's Paul would be willing to change her or his life for us—depends upon a deeper truth. That profound reality is that we are "forgiven" of that dimension of our past we have come to regret. Right before Jesus breathed his last for us on the cross, he reassured the repentant thief, "This day you will be with me in Paradise" (Luke 23:43). Some may say that this is to invoke a religious truth to reach one's personal truth. But of course it is. Jesus endured the worst that institutional power can visit upon a person as an act of divine forgiveness for each of us that no institution can ever deny us. If God the Father thought enough of us to let his beloved Son Jesus undergo this, then we are forgiven and can start to believe in the affection that our Sally or Paul may show us. Our search for paradise ends and begins with this ultimate truth that sets us free in our own soaring significance. We don't need Carl's AT-6 to open our horizons; the star of Bethlehem is truth enough.

- 8 -

What Is Failure Anyway?

SHE WAS AS GENTLE AS HER GAELIC NAME. SHE HAD THAT STRAIGHT-forward honesty of her German heritage and the venturesome spirit of her Irish ancestry. It was a seemingly small kindness she did me in letting me share her book for needed study when I was far from home. But welcoming me into her "space" was a spot of sunshine in what up to then had been a somber month of solitude. I asked her age and she said 20. But that was just information. Deirdre then entrusted me with her truth: "Turning 20 was difficult for me." So simple, yet it spoke wisdom.

The late teens are our pivotal and wonderful years. It is a time when the whole world is open to us, when our choices are totally un-encumbered. It is a time when we are marvelously free of the stereo-typed prejudices that can dun us later under the guise of "in crowd" sophistication. At 17, we can't be bothered with such "pseudo chic" when there are so many solid appeals calling us to become ourselves in full spontaneity. At 16, we bid farewell to adolescence; at 17, we assume total responsibility for who we are. My young friend had the keen insight to see the value of those years just before 20. We were in Alsace-Lorraine at the time and her remark made me think back along the corridor of history to those French teenagers who are the glory of their heritage. Diane de Poitiers was still a teen when she became Queen of France. Mary Stuart was still a teen when she became Queen of Scotland. Joan of Arc was a mere 18 when she routed the English and saw the Dauphin crowned at Rheims. No wonder the powers-that-be wanted to imprison her for life: Joan had too much spontaneity for their rigid categories. They simply couldn't believe in such exploits coming from a teenager dressed in jeans and leading an army of men. But Joan would have none of their suppressive condescension. She preferred death to life imprisonment and was gone at 19—and has lived ever since in the heart of every French man and woman. Jean Anouih called her "the lark."

Perhaps it was a touch of Joan that Antoine de Saint Exupéry saw in the face of his host's niece. (During the Battle of France in 1940, St-Ex had lodged with a farmer's family near St-Dizier.) The gracious expression of that teenager became for St-Ex good enough reason for him to risk his life for France: "I returned from my mission over Arras, having formed my bond with my farmer's niece. Her smile became the crystal in which I could see my village and beyond my village, my homeland."[1] A teen had been the inspiration of France for centuries. St-Ex nearly names the teen in his life, whose smiling countenance was with him when he was lost in action over France in the summer of '44. It was the teenager's spirit of openness to the future that had kept him wary of the barriers that "prudent consideration" tends to set up:

> It is important to act in terms of a goal that is not clear at the outset. This has to do with the Spirit, not the intellect. It is the Spirit that prompts such love, but it is asleep . . . To be tempted is to be tempted when the spirit is asleep to yield to intellectual reasons.[2]

Teen-agers search out their particular goals in the spirit of unrestricted spontaneity. Then they encounter the "categorical" logic of academic advisors in college who demand that they declare their "major" by the end of freshman year (when Deirdre was still 18). Nowadays these counselors are under heavy pressure from career development officers, who see the primary purpose of college as proximate training for a job. Why do these officials insist that our young adults pin down their careers so early? Their conventional refrain: to secure a position! There it is: searching personal fulfillment is weighted down by the logic of getting good employment "with pension benefits"—at the ripe old age of 21! Freedom to find oneself versus economic security. No wonder my young friend had been reluctant to encounter the stifling smog of the pragmatic point of view that afflicts even our best liberal arts institutions.

The liberal arts are meant to open out the possibilities of personal freedom as we investigate their engaging expression in literature, philosophy, and the other humanities. But for whatever cultural reasons, schools of business have cropped up and have taken the high ground on many a liberal arts campus. Of course, training for business is a worthy and necessary pursuit. Of course, developing our skills for later employment as an accountant or computer programmer is important. (Whether this necessarily has to be done on a university campus is open to question: It's one thing for college athletic programs to be the "farm-system" for professional football and baseball teams; for liberal arts colleges to be "boot-camp" for the "Big 6" accounting firms is quite another, unless all their clients are to be accountants!) For career training is a means to an end and can never replace the essential pursuit of discovering the image of personal value with which each person can fully identify without the intrusion of other considerations.

Gainful employment, if you will, is a means to personal fulfillment in freeing us for the total élan of our living. That for James Galway is playing the flute. This had been the expression of his personal spirit long before he reaped the financial rewards in concerts and record sales that followed upon his television appearances. James Galway did not become a flutist to make money: this would have been a rank confusion of means and values. He himself put it best when he said that he was glad to be earning enough money not to have to worry about it. Money is a means for living well; to make it an end in itself is to put one's personal worth beyond oneself. James Galway would still be a fine flutist even if he had to earn food and shelter for his family by setting bricks. His fellow countryman Sean O'Casey was a railroad clerk by day and wrote his plays when he got home at night. Few outside his family knew what was in Sean's bank account at his death; but his plays keep as his own personal expression. His job as clerk was his living; his plays were his life. Sean had taken a job with Irish Rail; but his plough was set for the stars—to invoke the title of his best-known play. Playwright J.B. Keane followed in this tradition: Tending bar in Listowel was his job; writing plays became his truth.

In the U.S., however, securing a position has become the mark of success. Not just a job, but a position. What's the difference? A job is a way of earning a living. A position is more: beyond financial gain, it puts a person on the ladder towards an important post in his or her company. Being a check-out girl at a supermarket or a mail clerk is a job; being a lawyer for a prestigious firm is a position. We praise someone for having a powerful position in a brokerage house or an automobile company. Notice the words we use: *securing* a position that can lead to a *powerful* post. The description is inherently defensive: We secure a position in the face of strong competition from other applicants and we attain positions of power in our firm by outgaining others. These are seemingly aggressive terms. Yet, in the world of competition where our success can turn to failure with the latest corporate cutback, we hold our positions of power with a careful eye upon the factors that could undermine our standing. The tactics may be aggressive but the motives are still those of personal security, which is basically defensive. Self-protection always is! It makes us assume a functional attitude towards others in the company. This was the lesson Mary Cunningham learned from her painful experience as executive assistant to the chairman of the Bendix Company. She talks about it in her appropriately-named book *Powerplay*:

> For men, the emphasis has been more on careers. I'm quite content being a nurturer and believing in so many of those human values commonly attributed to women. But applied in the corporate world, these same values can work against us— unless we are careful, and I wasn't careful enough . . . Men seem intuitively to take a more practical approach. Many care about being "right"—but they also want to get the job done. And they don't view defeat as anything glorious, no matter how noble the cause. I'm not sure I'd want to trade pragmatism for virtue, but a harmonious blend might do some good.[3]

Mary Cunningham is an Irish Catholic woman who payed the price of success in corporate America. She alludes to the need men have to be a success in their chosen enterprise and the sense of failure that stalks them if they fall short. This was the shadow over Irish Catholic John Cleary's existence as we meet him in Frank Gilroy's play, *The Subject Was Roses*. John, in his own mind at least, could have been a business success if he had taken the position in Brazil his coffee company had offered him. But his wife Antoinette wouldn't leave New York City. So John makes the daily rounds on his sales route, just as he has for the past 20-odd years, without much in the way of wealth to show for it. But he's full of pride for his son Tim who has just mustered out of service after World War II. John had volunteered for the Army during the First World War but was turned down because he was the sole support of his mother and family. That was another chance at being a success that had slipped John by. He would have basked in Tim's wartime exploits, but his son quickly lets him know that there had been no heroism in his military record.

Why was John so keen in finding significance in something so external to him as his son's war experience? Simply put, his work had become a grind and his marriage to Antoinette had fallen flat. He could have handled not becoming a highly-paid executive with his company if he could have found personal fulfillment in his homelife. But Nettie had not been willing to change her life for John, not even to share his delight in the summer cottage he had surprised her with. That had been the symbol of "home" for John and he had carefully marshaled his earnings to buy it "on time." Nettie had shot down that symbol like a duck over the lake it bordered: John and Timmy could go out and stay in it but she would still spend most Sundays with her mother in the Bronx. John's world with Nettie collapsed on him that day. There was no longer any home life for John: it was now a matter of making enough commission on his coffee sales to pay the apartment rent and provide Nettie with food and household money.

The gray routine of John and Nettie's daily existence had become strictly functional. Shatter the symbols of belonging and a person is shorn of reference points for his or her unique significance in the eyes of a friend. That was John's plight in life with his wife. Nettie had a puritan streak as bleak as that of Oliver Cromwell, for all her Catholic upbringing. Her horizons had narrowed to household economics and any affection she might have once felt for John had long since been diverted to the "safe" outlet of raising Timmy. She had refused her husband sexual union since the death of their infant John Jr.—whatever her reasons, perhaps a fear of personal intimacy. (Nettie acknowledges to Timmy: "He was not like my father at all . . . I was attracted . . . and I was afraid. I've always been a little afraid of him . . ."[4]) She is critical of John and Timmy's drinking too much at

Timmy's homecoming party. And the apparent gift of "roses" from John touches Nettie only because these had been the birthday remembrance her father had always given her. In a sense, Nettie had never really married because she had never formed home with John: the man in her life had remained her father even after his death. After once again resisting John's amorous approaches and throwing the vase of roses on the floor as her sign of refusal, Antoinette repeats a remembered dialogue to herself: "Who loves you, Nettie? . . . "You do, Papa." . . . "Why, Nettie?" . . . "Because I'm a nice girl, Papa."[5] Her devotion to her father was laced with a strong trace of the Manichaean put-down of sexual expression. John, with his energy and "a certain wildness," could never match the standard of her father who, for Nettie, was "the kindest, gentlest man who ever lived."[6]

But Antoinette was not kind. She had made John feel wrong for wanting to express love for her in a sexual way. John may have had a little too much to drink but it was Nettie who sinned. (John admits to Antoinette that if he hadn't had a couple of drinks under his belt, he wouldn't have had the courage to ask her to make love with him.) Since belonging in relationship is personal fulfillment, sin is whatever does damage to such a relationship. Nettie does great harm to John by making him feel guilty for desiring sexual union with her.

But it wasn't just in sexual matters that Nettie had a way of making John feel guilty. She had made him squirm for not taking a day off to take Timmy to the ballgame. She does the same to her son in making Tim feel guilty for not wanting to go over right away to visit his handicapped cousin Willis. Nettie's sin is in manipulating her husband and son through the sense of guilt she lays upon them for not adhering to her own particular notion of duty. Nothing does more damage to spontaneous relationships in family and friendship than making our beloved do our bidding by subtly tugging at their affection for us and making them feel they are letting us down if they don't comply. John Macmurray points up the harm that comes of such imposition: "The sense of guilt isolates a man from his fellows because it carries with it the feeling that his fellows have a right to punish him."[7] This sense of isolation is what no friend, child, parent or spouse would ever visit upon his or her beloved, no matter how pressing the engagement or keen the disappointment to oneself that is at stake.

Nettie was caught in the despair of making something a duty that she could not count upon the other doing out of spontaneity. This says more of herself than it does of Tim or John. She was staving off the sense of insignificance that had descended upon her the day Timmy had gone off to service. Since neither John nor Nettie expressed appreciation for one another, their relationship had become a functional arrangement rather than a shared union of total friendship. Nettie found her significance in raising Tim. John found his in keeping the paychecks coming in. But neither spouse felt fully adequate in his or her function. Nettie was sensitive to John's criticism of her for babying Tim. John was bothered by Nettie's nagging him for more cash. So they reacted to the feelings of inadequacy under the other's scrutiny by protecting their respective "turf." Nettie's haven of defense was her mother's home in the Bronx where the Sunday visits had become all the more vital for her, with Tim in the army. John's lay in the secret of his bank account balance. Both parents reveal these sensitivities when Tim comes home. Nettie breaks down and cries because she burns Tim's waffles—she had so wanted to live up to her significance as mother and keep him at home for good with scrumptious breakfasts. John becomes vociferously annoyed when Tim asks him how much he has in his savings account. That cushion against the future and symbol of significance was John's business and his alone!

Such defensiveness can lead to violent outbursts at times, which it did between John and Antoinette after their night out with Timmy. The spiral had started with Nettie's refusal of John's marital advances that ended with her heaving the rose vase to the floor. When Tim later asks John what had prompted his mother's flare-up, John—still smarting under Nettie's rejection—employs a vulgar expression by way of reply. Tim reacts by calling his father "a pig," whereupon John slugs him. Deep hurt all around with vulgarity compounding the violence. But the storm is past by morning and it is Tim who clears the air.

John is first to apologize as he shares the sum in his bank account with his son. Tim is now conscious that in the past he and his mother had teamed up on his father, making John feel in the wrong. But the greatest emptiness Tim feels in his own life is that his father had never said "I love you." Fortunately, the 21-year-old is close enough to the honesty of his late teens to realize that he for his part had never told his father that he loved him. Tim does so there and then—before his mother comes back into the kitchen. John, fighting back the tears, embraces his son. John sheds his functional attitude at the last in expressing his appreciation of all that his son means to him in one brief gesture. In that moment of vulnerability, the real John emerges who no longer has to prove himself to anybody, least of all his son. Whether John's newly-found appreciation attitude will break the impasse with Antoinette the play doesn't go on to say. But at its finish, John with Nettie's acquiescence sets his son free to discover significance in his living. He will not crowd his son's space to search out his own star. John breaks the cycle that would lay upon his son his own feelings of inadequacy and the tensions with his wife. Both Tim and Nettie are aware of John's complete sincerity because of his complaint about the morning coffee—his code for feeling fine.

John had let go his tenacious clinging to the need to be a success and the need to be right, in knowing that his son accepted him just as he was—bull-headed, brusque, volatile in his moods and completely generous at heart. But Tim had to practically scream his plea of "Listen to me" to get John to attend to his son's deeply-felt appreciation for him. John had started the day with his apology to Tim for having hit him and disclosing his long-guarded financial worth. But it was too much like going to confession at St. Francis Church—turning over a new slate, with John doing all the talking. He was even setting the conditions of their reconciliation by asking Tim to admit he too had made a mistake in wanting to leave home and live on his own. But such deténte would have kept father and son on good terms—but still apart. Fortunately for John, Tim was able to get through to his father. In listening to his son, John had found the truth he'd been looking for all his adult life: he did not have to be a success; he did not have to fit the format of business or even church guidelines. His faults and failures were not the last word about himself. Tim was a friend who could get beyond these external matters to John's inner worth as a person, who was lovable just as he was. In real life, Mary Cunningham found the lovable side of her former boss Bill Agee when he too let go the need to image himself as an invincible leader in the corporate world:

> Had he not become less of a hero, less of a *wunderkind* and more of a person, I don't know that I ever could have fallen in

love with him. It was the whole process of shared pain and
recovery that brought us close. I lost an idol but I gained a
friend, a true friend, a person capable of weakness and therefore a person who could be loved.[8]

Power, wealth, success—making these the preoccupation of our living
can blind us to those true friends who would appreciate us if we didn't
have a dime to our name.
To put our significance in power introduces the dread of weakness. To put our significance in wealth introduces the dread of poverty. To put our significance in success introduces the dread of failure.
Why do we do that? Why do we place our personal significance in
externals like wealth and power that are beyond ourselves? Burl Ives
as millionaire Big Daddy in the movie version of Tennessee Williams'
Cat on a Hot Tin Roof puts the lie to these as symbols of *personal*
significance. "Mendacity" he calls them in the trenchant scene with his
son Brick in the basement of their Southern mansion. Big Daddy was
dying of cancer and he knew that even as he talked, other members of
the family were upstairs plotting out the positions of power they
would inherit upon his death. That's why he points to the basement
full of antiques his wife had accumulated in umpteen trips to Europe
as "mendacity"—as hollow as the feigned concern for his health that
masked the grasping for a slice of his holdings. Big Daddy gets so
worked up that he goes weak and has to sit down. Relaxed now, he
tells his son (played by Paul Newman) about his own father who had
been a hobo traveling from place to place in boxcars, taking his young
son with him. His heart had given out running for one of those trains
and all he left his son was a beat-up suitcase. But he died with a
smile on his face—Big Daddy catches a tear crossing his eye in remembrance. Then Brick pulls his father up short with the question, "Is
that all he left you? He gave you love and he died with a smile on his
face because he was so happy to be with you!" It's Big Daddy's turn
to drop pretension: "I guess you're right, son; I still miss that old man.
'spect that the last happy moment I had on this earth was with him."
    Big Daddy finally admits his truth. He had known happiness
only with the one person he could count upon loving him. And that
man was a failure. No power. No money. But he had a son to whom
he had given all the love in his heart. And being poor and powerless

in those meager days of the early 30s, his dad was not distracted from being with his son. Big Daddy had forgotten something along the way: that you don't need to be a success to have a person love you. But "making something of ourselves" can blur that truth in shadowing the horizon of our future with the cloud of losing out. The dread of failure can fuel the drive to success so intently that we do not appreciate or may not even be aware of the love that others offer us if we took time to look. Ironically, it was the suffering his own father had endured in his poverty that had prodded Big Daddy to strive for success. Being an orphan can itself be a strong stimulant to work hard for one's place in the world. It did this for Tom Monaghan, who parlayed the earnings from his Domino Pizza chain into ownership of the Detroit Tigers baseball team. (To his credit, Tom never forgot those who had befriended him and taken him in—the nuns at his orphanage.) Big Daddy, like so many real-life orphans, had not been so fortunate. Life became so harsh for him in his youth that years later he would acknowledge that love had gone out of his life when his dad had died. He felt people were impressed with him for his accomplishments rather than for himself. Sadly, Big Daddy did not take a chance on finding out whether anyone else but his dad could love him for himself until he was dying of cancer. Then it was the son he had been hardest on who stuck by him like Cordelia for Shakespeare's Lear. At the finish, Big Daddy was blessed to realize the sincere honesty and affection of that son. The final failure of death has a way of straightening out the meaning of success and failure in flushing out "mendacious" trappings and false friends.

All too late Big Daddy had come to the genuine values in living that a French actress spoke of in a rare interview: "For me my family is the most beautiful memory I keep from my past life. Since I no longer have family, I realize that nothing can replace them . . . I have always lived as I yearned to—naturally, simply, with a need to please, to love and be loved."[9] No wonder Charles de Gaulle praised this actress, Brigitte Bardot, for her "sterling simplicity." She had kept herself free of the fixation on success that can clutter the spirit of a person with anxieties about failure.

To make life pleasant for others, to love and to be loved says it all—and that's what Big Daddy's own father had done. A life of hardship can be soothing to our inner heartstrings because of the sharing.

A life of comfort can corrode the spirit, as Brigitte's own countryman Antoine de Saint Exupéry wrote in his notebook: "Happiness does not rest in consumer items and the person who lets sterile attachment to his Ferrari get in the way of friendship is really hoodwinked."[10]

> St-Ex echoes Jesuit Albert Delp who wrote his own "*carnets*" (notebooks) in his prison cell before his execution by the Nazis:[11] He wondered if Christians in helping the poor out of their poverty were not using upper middle-class affluence as the norm. Delp felt that in employing an external measure of success we actually rob the poor of that sense of inner worth which is the authentic basis for all Christian endeavor. He may have been on to something; a former U.S. program for the poor was even called "Upward Bound"!

Making something of ourselves has for years meant being "upwardly mobile." But in the last decade so many young adults made their mark in the computer industry and Wall Street "arbitrage" that an initial was added—giving us the quite common noun *yuppie* (young upwardly mobile professional person). Though the Stock Exchange crumble of October '87 put a crimp in the ascent, the yuppie profile has been the image of success circulating in our colleges and universities for a generation. Through a quirk in the history of our "semi-conductor" age, the breakthrough in the computerization of America came at the hands of very young entrepreneurs and produced a raft of millionaires under age 40.

This dazzling history of accomplishment has its dark side in the soaring rate of suicide among American youth ranging from age 16 to 25. Making the yuppie the image of the "successful" graduate from our suburban high schools and our colleges has increased the dread of failure of those so near in age to these "golden boys" yet so far from being ready to meet the artificial pressures of making it in the market. Stripping our high schools and colleges of the liberal arts has left our young without much opportunity to probe the meaning of personal worth and human values beyond the "bottom line" preoccupation with profit and loss.

Yes, the stress upon financial and professional success can be traced right back to our highschools and colleges with their current concentration upon career training. Our most dedicated superintendents and deans are checkmated in their concern to have the course of studies reflect emphasis upon the humanities and wisdom rather than on careers and moneymaking. By whom? Often enough by the more vocal parents of the students themselves. It is this *parental* dread of failure that is compounded and laid upon the children at an age when the students should be opening up the vistas of their own futures with growing confidence. This image of success, imposed upon them from without, with the attendant pressures to "achieve," traps too many of our young people in the pits of despair that some escape via drugs or suicide.

The real-life hobos of the 30s portrayed by Big Daddy's father also had a passel of problems facing them in life which sent many to the bottle. But you don't read of their taking their own lives in the shocking numbers of our "stressed-out" young of today. That may have been because few people in the 30s could look to financial wealth or power as a measure of success. Being of modest means was no reason to feel inferior. Nor was there shame in being out of work, with so many plants closing. *"Hard Times"* was the name Studs Terkel gave his book covering that era. But they were good times too, as Big Daddy remembered in the smiling face of his dad.

What does failure mean anyway? Doesn't it come down to this: that a person hasn't achieved the level of living that was set for him or her by others? We may like to think that we set our own standards in this matter—but then, why do we feel shame in falling short of our goals? What difference does it make, unless we can't help glancing over our shoulders for the reaction of others—"to see how we played in Peoria?" No, the need to be recognized goes back to our childhood elation in the pride of our parents as we rode our two-wheeler down the walk without landing in the bushes. We want to succeed because it pleases those who mean most to us. And if what we do displeases them, sadness crosses our heart, much as we may disguise it with a chuckle. Our parents instilled those small norms for personal achievement that were necessary for our personal growth. We appreciated this because they had presented these goals to us in the context of affection. We weren't sent to our room because we flopped on our red bike and broke a spoke. They still spoke to us.

However, the hard economic realities of today practically force parents to insist upon their children doing well in school. Before World War II, a college education was not a prerequisite for entering

the world of business. Before World War II, there was little pressure
for a woman to have a college education since as wife and mother she
would remain at home. That has all changed with a large percentage
of married women currently working outside the home, with many others raising their children as single parents. So parents of today are
necessarily concerned that their children get a good education in
school, especially since the farm and factory employment of Big
Daddy's era has become so sparse in our service-oriented nation. But
that's all the more reason why parents must resist conveying any sug-
gestion that they love their children less for not making it to college or
for having to settle for a job rather than a position!

Parents must not set the "star" for their children but let each
know that their own dreams are fulfilled in having had "the wonderful
life" with their sons and daughters at home until they turned 20. Bona
fide parental love is not conditioned upon the child's accomplishments. The child never ceases being the son or daughter of the father
and mother so that the adult who was once the child still carries the
image of his or her own worth and lovableness instilled by the parents.
Up until about fifth grade in school, the child feels that he (she) can
count on his parents' love no matter what. But then the pressure hits
as he feels inferior or that he is letting his parents down because of
getting poor grades in math and English composition. The boy begins
to feel less lovable for falling down in school work. He now feels he
has to "earn" back the love of his parents by "doing better." And if he
just isn't cut out for academic achievement at the age of 10 (why a
child has to peak academically so early remains a mystery), he may
turn to playing baseball or the clarinet to impress his parents in other
ways. The pressure along this line becomes greater in high school,
where he feels he has to earn the attentions of his girl-friend and classmates by his feats, if not in the classroom, then on the playing field.
His parents are the only people who ever loved him for himself and
now even they seem to have conditioned his lovableness upon performance. Since no one else could possibly love him for himself, he
now has to impress others with signs of his accomplishment.

Parents do hold the key to the child's feeling of acceptance because the son or daughter now in high school knows that once upon a
time Mom and Dad had loved him or her without reservation. Then
with the advent of house chores and schoolwork, the parents seemed to

stress achievement so much that the child began to feel he or she had to earn Mom and Dad's love.

A faulty image of personal value can come out of such experiences: that only our parents could ever love us for ourselves and that we have to earn the love of anyone else by making a good impression. This could explain why Antoinette Cleary had never totally given her love to her husband, John. Her father was the only person in her life who could possibly love her for herself. And even he had subtly set a condition for his devotion—that Nettie never let a man get close to her sexually because that wasn't nice. So for Antoinette sexual relations in marriage were the duty of the wife, rather than the spontaneous expression of total love for her spouse. In her own mind, Nettie had to earn the respect of John and the affection of Tim by making a good home for them.

John, in his own way, was burdened with the same narrow image of personal value. Ironically, it was the recruiting office that had canonized his mother's love for him in barring him from the Navy to be her support. Just as the "cult" to father-love had kept Nettie from the completely open embrace of John as her beloved, the tie to mother-love had prevented John from following his "star." He never quite surmounted his sense of inadequacy for not having proved himself a "man" in wartime service. He felt he had to earn the love of others by being a success. He too never thought he could be loved for himself but only for the accomplishments he could point to. But there were no trophies or medals in his trunk.

Nettie indeed had been taken with John's youthful good looks, his vitality, and his ambitions for the future, which is why she married him. He had made a good impression. But he had not lived up to his economic promise, either in her eyes or in his own. So the impression had worn off and little love or tenderness had carried over from Nettie's devotion to her father to John. Even after his death, roses had meaning only in terms of her cult to her father that no other could touch. In making her father God, Antoinette had excluded John from the focus of her living. A true providence, however, freed John from the chilly impasse of his home life. Tim's spontaneous expression of affection convinced John that he was lovable and that he no longer had to impress his son or his wife with the success he might have been. In a paradoxical turnabout, it was the child who relieved the parent of the need to be a success. If the memory of his father's love amidst misery had finally brought Big Daddy back to his lost sense of being lovable just as he was, Tim's putting his affection in words had dispersed the cloud of failure that had ever haunted John Cleary.

If a person tries to make life pleasant for others, if a person loves and is loved, there is no failure. Small-time Chicago gangster "Artful Eddie" O'Hare would seem to have died a failure. But he was loved by his sixteen year old son Edward, Jr. "Butch," as his father called him, wanted to go to Annapolis—being a U.S. Navy pilot was his "star." The difficulty was that entrance to the Naval Academy was by Congressional appointment only. Artful Eddie was quite aware that when the local congressman checked Butch's' background, his father's association with the Chicago underworld would surface and the application would be denied. Artful Eddie wasn't about to let that happen. So he turned himself into the police, knowing full well that the mob would "blow him away." Which they did—but not before his son was admitted to the Naval Academy. The notice in *The Chicago Tribune* would mark Artful Eddie's passing as that of just another local mob crony who died as he lived—a failure. His son, Edward "Butch" O'Hare became the first Navy pilot to receive the Congressional Medal of Honor for bravery in World War II. He died for his country over Tarawa in the South Pacific in 1943. Butch gave his all, as had his dad. Chicago's international airport is named for Butch, but O'Hare Field could also stand for Artful Eddie who had taught his son there is no failure where there is love. At the finish the man crucified on Calvary as a criminal had only the support of his mother and two loyal friends: one a fisherman, the other a former prostitute. But he was no more a failure than Artful Eddie. Jesus lived as he always yearned to: naturally, simply, with a need to make life pleasant for others, to love and be loved. What is failure anyway?

- 9 -

The Down-and-Out Corner of Kindness

"WILL YOU, TOO, GO AWAY?" JESUS DIRECTS THIS MOST POIGNANT line in the Gospels to his twelve after his rejection by the townspeople of Capernaum. Peter turns spokesman but doesn't quite answer: "To whom shall we go? You have the words of eternal life." Yet Peter would deny even knowing Jesus in the hours following Christ's arrest, and was absent from Calvary. Peter had gone away. So Jesus' loneliness was compounded on Calvary. Being abandoned by the friend a person counted on most can do that. In viewing Matthias Gruenewald's depiction of Jesus' last hours, we are taken with the presence of Mary his mother, Mary Magdalene and John at the foot of the cross. But their company did not keep Jesus from crying out, "My God, My God why hast thou forsaken me?" We can have the support of all those who mean most except one. And that one may be the person who occupies the most cherished corner in our heart, the one we keep looking for out of the corner of our eye. We are grateful for the attention of the rest but the absence of our best friend in our critical moment is saddening.

There is no failure where there is love: but there is gnawing desolation in being let down by a friend. No wonder Jesus had gasped, "I thirst." It wasn't just the physical pain that was doing him down. He was feeling the loss of the company of a friend. It reminds of Macmurray's remarks about the cry of an infant: "The baby's cries convey, not some organic distress, but simply the need for the mother's presence to banish the sense of loneliness, and to reassure

107

him of her care for him."[1] The need for a drink in an hour of distress goes back to our infancy and the solace we sought at our mother's breast when the shadow of isolation closed around us. Émile Zola intimates this in *L'Assommoir* where he describes the "still" as if it were the maternal bosom "that was so comforting."[2]

It is very curious that the same puritan streak in Christianity that curbs the show of tenderness as immature also prohibits alcoholic beverages. Curious too that we reject this distortion of what Jesus stood for as we continue to toast our weddings with champagne, salute our birthdays with cordials, and bury our dead with a shot of brandy to settle our nerves. (Irish Americans had the custom of setting out a bottle of Irish whisky with a shot glass on a green flannel cloth with a guest's morning coffee: I think that's a neat gesture but then I've always taken my drinks neat.) We cannot help but celebrate the key moments in our lives with glad affection and the wine of conviviality, even as Jesus did at Cana. This all makes sense in view of our primordial experience of belonging in our mother's affectionate embrace and our first calming nourishment at her breast. It may also account for the solace many humans seek in drink in the face of indictment or rejection by family or friend for guilt or failure.

The alcoholic overwhelmed by his sense of abandonment and condemnation takes "flight into illness" to draw the maternal attention he knew as a sick child. That was Larry Shannon's way of blocking out his past and securing the attentions of Maxine as we meet him in Tennessee Williams' *The Night of the Iguana*. Her run-down tourist hotel in Mexico was where Larry would "crack up on schedule," never failing to attract the ministrations of this unlikely nurse. Williams' play is a take-off on Malcolm Lowry's novel, *Under the Volcano*, whose central character is a Canadian consul instead of a suspended Anglican priest Larry Shannon. In a sense, the novel is more interesting than *The Night of the Iguana* because it deals directly with the connection between the consul's sense of abandonment by his wife and his mirage of alcoholic fantasy. Lowry, himself an alcoholic, was able to describe events the way a person "under the influence" sees them. The novel is as hard to follow as an alcoholic's train of thought but includes sometimes brilliant revelations of the upside-down world he finds himself in: "The carousel swirling in the town plaza was like my life—offering me one more chance to leap on the platform before the music stopped."[3]

Maxine's hacienda was Shannon's chance to get off the merry-go-round in his life that kept circling back on him. He never could seem to escape the chase of those who would make him wrong. They were always at his heels. The prosecutors this time were a busload of Baptist women for whom he had been acting as tour-director. Except that he somehow had mismanaged their funds and had herded them into some scruffy taco diners for meals. He had even changed their itinerary to lodge at Maxine's place. It wasn't just his boozing that bothered the Baptist contingent. Charlotte, the precocious high-schooler in the group, had become infatuated with his elegant manners and handsome looks. Shannon couldn't resist his irresistibility in this girl's eyes, so when he discovered her in his room at the last stop, he had soothed his loneliness with an all-night tryst. This puts him in deep trouble as the group leader, Miss Fellowes, calls the tourist headquarters to have him fired immediately.

The scenario of guilt and condemnation was familiar to him, so this time he anticipates his fall from grace by making sure it would occur at Maxine's. Shannon was certain that she wouldn't throw him out. She was as lonely as he and for similar reasons. She had long since given up finding anyone who could love her for herself. Like Shannon, she has attempted to cover the emptiness of not belonging to someone with rum-colas and sexual liaisons. She's blunt about it: "I know the difference between loving someone and just sleeping with someone—even I know about that."[4] Shannon and Maxine each portray the self-defeat Harry Guntrip talks about: "When we fail to achieve genuinely personal relationships, . . . we may substitute appetitive gratifications instead, and then the appetitive compulsion symbolizes our reaching out after personal relationship, as is conspicuously the case in sexual compulsions."[5] Maxine's self-esteem came apart when her late husband Fred lost interest and preferred fishing to her company. By her own admission, his conversation with her had dwindled to a few "grunts" of nay and yea per day. Even her taking up with the Mexican porter raised nary a nod of approval or disapproval from Fred before his quick death. Their relationship had succumbed long before Fred.

Shannon's despair goes back to his mother. Her affection for him had ceased abruptly when she had come upon his self-eroticism. Hairbrush in hand, she punished the youngster there and then to warn him of the dire punishment God would visit upon him if he continued the practice. Condemned by his mother and her God, Shannon had no one to turn to by way of refuge. Whether Shannon had become an Anglican clergyman to earn back God's love, Williams does not indicate. But Shannon is turned out of his church less than a year after ordination for seducing his young secretary and for his sermon dismissing the judgmental God of Calvin as a senile old man. Both lapses in the playwright's delineation were Shannon's extreme reaction to his mother's taking away her love and putting him under the ruthless judgment of her Manichaean God, who would condemn him for his coming-of-age sexually. (After his poignant *The Glass Menagerie*, Tennessee Williams rarely reverted to understatement to make his point.)

True to Guntrip's profile, Shannon in his guilt before his mother and her God had given up on anyone loving him for himself; so he "was driven in desperation to clutch at physical contact" as a way of relieving his loneliness. And though just about every tour (Shannon had become a travel director after his suspension by the church) offered him this covert compensation, his guilt became more engrained with each sexual encounter and his feeling of isolation more desolate. If the relationship is based upon reciprocal self-gratification without the mutual love of friendship, it seals off deeper personal rapport beyond the mere sexual satisfaction that any partner can provide. If persons have sexual relations with one another before friendship is formed, the suspicion is already planted that self-gratification is the other's primary interest. Misgivings about ever being loved for oneself multiply even as the pain of isolation is driven deeper. Another woman comes upon the scene to point this out to Shannon. She is itinerant painter Hannah Jelkes, who arrives at the hotel with her aged poet of a grandfather. Hannah claims to be good at sketching eyes "looking in and looking out"; she is unerring in reading Shannon's riven soul:

> I was on the verandah this afternoon when the latest of these
> young ladies gave a demonstration of how lonely the intimate
> connection has always been for you. The episode in the cold,

inhuman hotel room, Mr. Shannon, for which you despise the
lady almost as much as you despise yourself. . . . Oh no, Mr.
Shannon, don't kid yourself that you travel with someone.
You have always traveled alone.[6]

Hannah is not admonishing Shannon but opening the way of release from the guilt that haunts him. She is simply calling his bluff
when he claims that he always has company. No, Hannah rejoins—
sexual partners, yes; the company of friends, no. Hannah is right on
the mark: Shannon had slapped Charlotte after their sexual interlude
and forced her to kneel with him to ask God's forgiveness. Shannon
was still chained to his mother's Manichaean God whose "spook" of
condemnation followed him everywhere. Maxine could not offer him
salvation because she hadn't been able to combine self-acceptance
with her need for sexual expression any better than Shannon. She had
been turned aside from any affection and marital embrace by her late
husband, "cool and decent" Fred. Maxine was now resigned to the
functional attitude in which she saw others and herself as acceptable
merely for their usefulness or delight—but never for the worth of oneself: "We've got to settle for something that works for us in our
lives— even though it's not at the highest kind of level."[7] But resort-
ing to sexual rendezvous and liquor hadn't built any self-esteem in
Shannon. They are forbidden in the eyes of the God of his mother that
he can't quite dismiss. The upshot is that he cannot cope with being
discharged by his tourist agency when his replacement comes upon the
veranda asking for the bus key. Shannon's frenzied protest at being
fired from his job with the "guilty" verdict of the Baptist busload becomes so bizarre that the Mexican valets have to tie him into the ham-
mock.

Shannon fully expects Hannah to mother him through this latest
flight to illness. She had befriended him and had earlier protected him
from entrapment by the Baptist leader and from the taunts of the Nazi
hotel guests. But she will not let him wallow in self-imposed expia-
tion as if punishment were to be his usual lot in life: "You're still
indulging yourself in your . . . Passion Play performance."[8] Hannah is
wedging Shannon away from the pit of self-pity, which is another ruse
to draw attention to oneself. Hannah refuses to let Shannon retreat
into the world of self, even to delight in punishing himself. She can

only bring him to belief in a merciful God and to her forgiveness as representative of that God if Shannon can look outwards from self. Hannah senses that Shannon, unlike Maxine who is enmeshed in the cynicism of her functional outlook, has a compassionate nature, as is evidenced in his concern and respect for her grandfather. She detects his need to believe in something, someone besides himself. She praises him for maintaining his decency towards others in spite of the cloud of condemnation that has bedeviled his life.

Hannah finds God in the eyes of old people like her grandfather, whose eyes glisten in their yearning for the kind regard of others and the reassurance of belonging. Hannah experiences God in communication between people, in "a little understanding exchanged between them, a wanting to help each other through nights like this."[9] Hannah's is a God of love for whom nothing is immoral or indecent except violence and deliberate unkindness. She will have no part in the glowering judgment of the righteous Baptist women that would deepen Shannon's sense of guilt. Nor will Hannah let the slavering Nazi tourists treat him as a "fool" for their delight—however hysterical Shannon's attempts to salvage some self-regard in his hour of condemnation.

The Baptist matrons had ignored and the obtuse Nazis had never known Jesus' strongest injunction: "If you call your brother "fool," you will suffer the fires of Gehenna." (Mt.5:22) But Hannah was keenly aware that all morality begins with self-respect, and that her God would accept all things human except the trampling upon the respect owed each person as son or daughter of God the Father. To make another human squirm under the glaring judgment of one's self-righteousness is the ultimate sin for Jesus: it would deny the dignity each person possesses as the beloved of the Father for sharing the humanity of Jesus. The "master race" in their idiotic ideology would make others feel inferior and rob them of respect—as Saint Exupéry wrote before he went to his death in ridding his homeland of this menace: "Respect for another person! This is the touchstone. When the Nazi respects exclusively the individual who resembles him, he is respecting nothing but himself."[10]

Hannah respected Shannon as someone other than herself in a way the Baptists could not. They were quick to condemn Shannon for his sexual rendezvous. Tennessee Williams intimates, however, that the motivation behind Miss Fellowes' prosecution of Shannon was jealousy: Shannon had diverted Charlotte's attentions away from her! The Baptists were so fixed upon Shannon's acquiescence in Charlotte's pursuit of him that they barely adverted to where the initiatives had originated. They had so little respect for Shannon as one different from themselves that it was easy for them to gloss over the nubile antics of their protegée and mask the ulterior motives of her mentor, Miss Fellowes. People have a way of blinding themselves to the truth of things under the cover of self-righteousness. So, no wonder Jesus would protect the woman caught in adultery in the face of the Pharisee jury: "Let him who is without sin among you be first to throw a stone at her." (John 8:7) Jesus would not let this religious group set themselves up in judgment over this daughter of the Father any more than Hannah would let the Baptist women sway her positive opinion of Shannon.

Hannah restores Shannon's self-esteem as she leads him to a sense of self-acceptance and forgiveness in the eyes of her kind God. But Shannon has a misgiving: How can Hannah be sure her God will not condemn him for his sexuality, if she herself has not had erotic experience? Would she still accept herself in the eyes of her God if she had? Hannah reassures Shannon in relating to him an incident in which she had been party to the erotic fantasies of a gentle, shy salesman she had met. Shannon dismisses the gesture as "dirty," but Hannah won't let him revert to the Manichaean narrowness with which he has ever indicted himself. Hannah insists, "Nothing human disgusts me unless it's unkind, violent."[11] Her noncarnal gesture was meant as an act of kindness to a terribly lonely man. At long last the merry-go-round in Shannon's life glides to a halt in the peace of Hannah's forgiveness.

Things have come full circle in the providence of Hannah's merciful God. Shannon's sense of being forgiven in "the truth that sets a person free," is symbolized by his cutting the rope that releases the iguana tied under the verandah. As the ugly animal scurries into the brush, Shannon's "spook" of condemnation disappears with it. Hannah had given him a cup of poppy tea to soothe his frayed nerves and sincere affection for his thirsting spirit. Hannah had discerned the decency and good heart of the man whom the Baptist ladies had written off as a lecher and a drunk. Shannon had shown gentility and respect for Hannah and her grandfather. Hannah had responded in kind. She had also gotten by Maxine's rude manner and perceived the widow's need for Shannon's company. Maxine asks Shannon to stay and help her run the hotel—though she can't help putting the request in a crass way. No matter. As Maxine and Shannon head down to the beach for a swim, Larry can be himself at last. If he should express love sexually with Maxine, it will not be desperate clutching for self-gratification nor the dire protest of a man under inexorable judgment. In the eyes of Hannah's forgiving God, his expression will be that of tenderness for Maxine whose sympathy he had always welcomed. And if he should take the drink that Maxine offers, it will not be to escape the despondency of failure but to celebrate the "new wine in new wineskins" of his new life in which he has nothing to hide. Shannon can accept himself completely in the eyes of Hannah's God. In now believing himself lovable for himself, he can let Maxine begin to image herself as a loving person and not just a sexual partner in her gift of self to Shannon. Hannah had not only restored dignity to Shannon but through him had brought hope into Maxine's life.

In the instant that Hannah sends them off for their swim, her grandfather finishes the poem that brings his own life to completion. Hannah prays, "Oh God, can't we stop now? Finally? Please let us. It's so quiet here now."[12] Good missionary of God's mercy that she is, her prayer is answered. Her grandfather is released from the slippages of age and nods his head in death. Hannah is alone but with a sense of belonging under the kind Providence she has always believed in. She will bury her grandfather in this peaceful spot, grateful that his shoulder had always been the place where she could "nest and rest, emotionally speaking." This minor romantic poet had not been heard from for two decades, and only his granddaughter would know of his final poem and the struggle that had been his to finish it "in time." But there was love in every line so her memory of his legacy would keep. His company had filled any need in her for the solace Shannon had sought; but her gratitude made her quite sympathetic for all those who might turn to the bottle in their loneliness, whether of failure or for a friend who is far, far away.

We don't know why John Mooney of the Bronx had turned to alcohol—failure or loss of a spouse, a friend. Or maybe his image of the person he had yearned to become had collapsed upon him. I remember this as a comment a student of mine had made in a paper he had written about Dylan Thomas, who died of alcoholism. He said that the poet had reminded him of his grandfather who, as a young man, had this great vision of the person he longed to become. But then he became trapped in the workaday world and dull routine of Manhattan living and had turned to the bottle as his dream faded into the woodwork of his apartment. The student repeated the same biography for his father and said at the end, "I don't want that to happen to me." That was 20 years ago and my first in teaching the course that prompted this book. I pray that in God's good providence this student, now a man of 40, may have realized his dream.

We don't know whether somewhere in his silent past, John Mooney may have seen his dream slip away. But his neighbors, the real-life Hannahs in this world, knew him for a kind man who lived his life alone. John Mooney wasn't that old, really, when he died but his alcoholism had weakened him. His could have been the expression of another Irishman grown fragile except in his way with words: "I'm like a well-worn bar of soap and I'm down to the thin part and I'm easily broken." John had broken down in death without any living relative, bank account or any accomplishment he could point to. But not even Jesus was buried in Potter's Field. So his neighbors did the final dignity for John, whose legacy was respect for others: they took up a collection so that after his funeral Mass he would have his own proper plot in the cemetery. This is important for an Irishman, if only to verify his shy way of proposing marriage, "How would you like to be buried with our family?" I would have gone to his funeral, had I known. I would have gone because my own grandfather, whom I was never blessed to know, was named John Mooney. Bronx John Mooney had led a somber existence at the finish but his neighbors had fathomed his worth. Peter Coutros did too and called his newspaper write-up of John, "An Obit for a Decent Man." John Mooney—and every other person who in Hannah Jelkes' words has had "to fight for his decency"—deserve that we give it here in full:

> Boiled down to stark essentials, the life and times of John Mooney would never make it to the obituary page because once you got past his name and the fact that he was 51 years old when he died last Friday night, there wasn't much grist for the biographic mill. For one thing, it's not likely you or the

person sitting next to you ever heard of John Mooney. Outside of his neighbors who dubbed him "The Mayor of Walton Avenue," he was known to very few people. He died broke, which could suggest a mixed blessing if you accept the idea that there are always a lot of relatives out there ready to litigate the hell out of a man's last will and testament. In Mooney's case, there are none: no names to be listed in that part of the obituary which lists the next of kin. But when it comes time for the priest to sprinkle holy water on John Mooney's casket in Christ the King Church today, he'll not lack for mourners. Eileen Smigiel will weep for him and so will her husband, Bill. They're the supers at 1184 Walton Ave., Bronx and for the last nine years they have befriended him on the good days and mothered him through the long dark nights of his addiction to alcohol.

When Tom Matthews looked in on Mooney last Friday in the latter's single-room domicile just behind the Smigiel's apartment and tried to interest him in a session of television watching, he found him dead of what was later determined to be a heart seizure.

"He's not going to Potter's Field," Mrs. Smigiel remembers crying through her tears.

"Ain't no way that's going to happen, not even if I have to take out a loan," her husband reassured her. But at noon yesterday, while his wife fed some of their seven youngsters and prepared others for school, Bill pulled out a loose-leaf book and showed a visitor pages full of the names of those who had enlisted themselves in the cause of keeping John Mooney out of Potter's Field. Alongside of the 141 names was a number denoting the amount of the person's contribution. A man who runs a gas station and who had met Mooney only four times gave $20. One contribution was for 17 cents, which was all the money the woman had in the house when Eileen Smigiel and Mrs. Henrietta Green and Mrs. Ada Thomas went knocking on doors.

Last Christmas, Mrs. Green's husband gave Mooney a coat to ward off the chill when the bottle ran low. He cherished the coat. But when Bill Smigiel went out and bought him some new duds, Mooney passed them along to somebody he regarded as more needy than himself. "Last Christmas," Mrs. Thomas recalled, "All the neighbors gave him plates and trays of holiday goodies. He couldn't bear to say no to anyone, so what he did was to accept everything very graciously and then he went out and took care of other people with the platters." Last night, in the Walter B. Cooke funeral home at E. Tremont Ave. and the Grand Concourse, his neighbors came to pay their respects to the man they called their mayor. He had watched over their kids, summoned them when he saw a meter maid approaching with pad in hand. Looking down on the deceased—who was wearing Bill Smigiel's best suit— Eileen's mother, Mrs. Margaret Bowen, whispered of her old pinochle pal, "Poor John never knew how much people loved him." Then, she joined his other friends to share his legacy of love.[13]

Tennessee Williams, speaking through Hannah Jelkes, was right about people finding God in seeing one another through difficult times. The Smigiels had helped John through many a lonely hour but his was the legacy of love. "I was a stranger and you brought me home—" (Mt. 25:35). Jesus had identified himself with John Mooney; the Smigiels' and his other neighbors' response of love to this kind man became a moment of God in their lives.

Leaving Home

NEW YORK'S ST. PATRICK'S DAY PARADE IS AS OLD AS THE STATUE of Liberty. If Bartholdi's "Lady" lifts the torch of welcome for all who leave home and country to come to America, the parade symbolizes their natural reluctance to do so. The kilted pipers play the Thomas Moore melodies that put the older Irish immigrants lining the route right back at their Ballytore or Cavan hearthside.

Leaving their native land was for most a necessity to earn the living that had escaped them at difficult turns in Ireland's history. Yet home is where "their hearts had ever been" since first their "Kathleen" had been their "bonnie bride." (Kathleen ni Houlihan is the symbol of Ireland herself.) So after the parade, they'll stop down at Jim Brady's Tavern for a pint and listen to Michael "Jesse" Owens sing *"The Leaving of Liverpool"* and *"Mary of Dunloe."* The music will carry them home again with the trace of a tear. The Irish brought with them their marvelous way with words. So it's the music that transports them back in time and space to Cobh or Klondalkin where Mom has set out the rasher, tea and biscuits for breakfast and a lark is singing in the green fields beside. Words become as dated as Shakespeare's plays, Edmund Burke's speeches, and, God save us, Thomas Moore's lovely lyrics. Music, however, goes right to our sensibilities that knows no time except our heartbeat reminding us to live. A Mozart Andante can move us as "tenderly" as a melody line of Nat "King" Cole. Music has a way of shifting us back across the sea of years to our childhood and family celebrations, even if the song be that of a thrush warbling in a Central Park tree—as poet T.A. Daly found one day:

Ah! the May was grand this mornin'!
Sure, how could I feel forlorn in
Such a land, when tree and flower tossed their kisses to
    the breeze?
Could an Irish heart be quiet
While the Spring was runnin' riot,
An' the birds of free America were singin' in the trees?
In the songs that they were singin'
No familiar note was ringin',
But I strove to imitate them an' whistled like a lad.
O! my heart was warm to love them
For the very newness of them—
For the ould songs that they helped me to forget—an' I
    was glad.

So I mocked the feathered choir
To my hungry heart's desire,
An' I gloried in the comradeship that made their joy my
own,
Til a new note sounded, stillin'
All the rest. A thrush was trillin'!
Ah! the thrush I left behind me in the fields about Athlone,
Where upon the whitethorn swayin',
He was minstrel of the Mayin',
In my days of love an' laughter that the years have laid
    at rest;
Here again his notes were ringin'!
But I'd lost the heart for singin'—
Ah! the song I could not answer was the one I knew the
best.[1]

The song Tom Daly could not answer was the song he knew the
best from his boyhood. His "eternal" love for his home had overwhelmed him. Daly had not regretted coming to America. He had done all
right here and had built a good life for his wife and children. Yet this
could not dim his appreciation for home. Perhaps that is both the
blessing of leaving home and the reason for our reluctance to go: our
appreciation of all home means. British writer Elizabeth Goudge
speaks these nuances beautifully in her book, *Gentian Hill*:

Home! It showed you its face when you sat quiet within it at
that moment when day was passing into night, but it could

only reveal its spirit, its eternal meaning, when you stood at a little distance, just turning to leave it or just returning to it, seeing it at that transition moment when a larger world was claiming or releasing you. It was always at these transition times, it seemed, when for a moment nothing owned you and you owned nothing, that you saw things so very clearly.[2]

Gareth O'Donnell had reached this transition point in Brian Friel's play, *Philadelphia, Here I Come.* Gar feels he must give up his small Donegal village to search his star in Philadelphia where his mother's sister lives. But this means leaving his widower father, the only parent Gar has ever known since his mother had died giving birth to him. Friel invites us into Gar's private thoughts and feelings on this last day at home through a second character who portrays the inner side of the quiet man the neighbors think they know. The playwright through this dramatic device gives us the complete picture of the 24-year-old who outwardly seems so confident of venturing forth into the unknown, yet inwardly wishes his silent father would just say something to keep him home. Critic Wilfred Sheed called Friel's play one of the truest ever to have come from Ireland. This praise is deserved for one reason: its focus is not the public person at all but the mélange of impressions and feelings at the core of Gar's being that gives us an insight into his responses to others.

The motives that are the springs of our actions lay hidden from the gaze of others. The novelist can dwell upon them because a book can relate our dreams and dreads like a private diary that we keep to ourselves. But drama is symbolic action on a public stage depicting the way people deal with one another in similar real-life situations. What Friel has done is to introduce a character who is dramatically invisible to the others on stage, yet vitally present to us. In word and gesture this "private Gar" lets us in on the memories and longings, the dreams and fantasies, the motives and reactions which are often the reverse of the outward manner of this polite and shy young man. The voice-over on a movie-sound track attempts to convey the same as the main character walks the street alone—like Stacey Keach's Mike Hammer—and talks to himself in the sanctuary of his thoughts and feelings. Brian Friel puts this inner person on stage. The device works precisely because it is on stage away from the photographic world of cement sidewalks; inside the theatre we allow the playwright his imaginative ways of representing the truth about ourselves. Friel's play is so true to the hidden currents of personal interaction that we relate equally well to both characters. We each bring a public and private side to our engagements with others. The poignancy of the play is that neither father nor son lets the other glimpse his genuine feelings at this moment of parting. For the son loves the father and the father loves the son: but the Irish often go mute when feelings run deep. (This probably goes back to my great-grandfather Lyons' time in the potato famine when he said goodbye to his mother, knowing he would never see her again. Such partings were multiplied by thousands as the young people left their homeland, where people were starving to death, for a chance at a new life in America. The situation was much too bleak for any chronicle; the finality of the separation much too profound for language.) But mutual appreciation is there—which is why Sheed was "right on" in commending Friel for exposing the truth of it—and the blight of it, for not being communicated to the person who most needs to hear it. Yet strange to say, both father and son were emotionally sincere in an Irish sort of way. John Macmurray, himself a Celt, points up the need for integrity in the matter of our feelings: else, we deceive ourselves at the core of our being and become insensitive toward others.[3]

Gar O'Donnell was indeed honest about his feelings—even to the extent of calling his dad "Screwballs" as he goes over in silent memory his appreciation of that happiest day when they went fishing together. A newspaper dating from his parents' honeymoon had cut through Gar's dismay at his dad's not saying anything to mark his son's final day at home. Gar had found the faded pages in his dad's suitcase he was to use for his journey. Their brown edges spoke volumes of how life had closed down round S.B. O'Donnell when his own "bonnie bride" Maire had been taken from him within a year of their wedding. If S.B. could not find words at Gar's parting, it was for the hurt his heart carried for his "snowy breasted pearl" since placing the flower upon her grave that shivering morning so long, long ago. John McCormack's recorded lines from the song of the quoted name above streamed the feelings S.B. could not express: "We laid her in the grave where the willows sadly wave . . . and I'm alone, all alone. . . ." The old newspaper had cracked open the shell of Gar's appreciation and let him cherish once again his own golden moment with his father:

> God—maybe—Screwballs— . . . do you remember—it was an afternoon in May—oh, fifteen years ago—I don't remember every detail but some things are as vivid as can be: the boat was blue and the paint was peeling . . . and you had given me your hat and had put your jacket round my shoulders because there had been a shower of rain. And you had the rod in your left hand . . . and maybe we had been chatting—I don't remember—it doesn't matter—but between us at that moment there was this great happiness, this great joy—you must have felt it too—it was so much richer than content—it was a great, great happiness, an active bubbling joy—although nothing was being said—just the two of us fishing on a lake on a showery day.[4]

Gar tries to nudge his dad's memory of the occasion by asking about the boat. But his father, now in his late 60s, is vague in his recollections. After the death of his Maire, S.B. had engaged Madge Mulhern as housekeeper to raise his young son. He himself had buried his sorrow in the routine of running the general store in Ballybeg, i.e., "small town" in Gaelic. It is Madge who reassures Gar that just because his father doesn't say much doesn't mean he doesn't have feelings. Madge is the "point of rest" (in Coventry Patmore's fine phrase for the still center of a play) to whom both S.B. and Gar turn to speak the feelings they can't quite bring themselves to express to one another. The moment that S.B. treasures was Gar's first day at school—decked out in his Sunday best and not wanting to leave his father's side:

> D'you mind, (Madge), you tried to coax him to go to school, and not a move you could get out of him, and him as manly looking, and this wee sailor suit as smart looking on him, and—and—and at the heel of the hunt I had to go with him myself, the two of us hand in hand, as happy as larks—[5]

The pity the play points up is that father and son did not exchange the moments that meant most to each. S.B., however, hints at the reason for his reticence about asking his son to stay home. Prosperity had left the small town and S.B.'s business had fallen off. There was little opportunity for Gar to make a good living in Ballybeg. As much as he loved his son and would miss him sorely, S.B. could not pin him to a fading enterprise. He simply had too much integrity to play upon Gar's affection to close down his son's future. In a reverse sort of way, S.B.'s silence was his sincerity that Gar would come to realize only later.

Gar's own interior plea was to recover the sense of belonging he had once known when his father had pulled his own hat down over Gar's ears to ward off the chill. Gar had felt as snug as a bug in a rug. Cozy. Warm amidst the rain. Gar never had the primordial experience of resting upon his mother's shoulder and feeding at her breast. So he sought the comfort of home at the threshold of his father's memory of a boat in a misty lake on a showery afternoon. When his approach falters, Gar resorts to the phonograph: He puts on the Andante movement of the Mendelssohn Violin Concerto to help him relive that moment of total happiness and soothe his regret at having lost close rapport with his father:

> Listen! . . . D'you know what the music says? It says that once upon a time a boy and his father sat in a blue boat on a lake on an afternoon in May, and on that afternoon a great beauty happened, a beauty that has haunted the boy ever since, because he wonders now, did it really take place or did he imagine it?[6]

Yet the only words he can prompt from his father, other than the usual refrain of checking the store stock, are comments about the rainy weather predicted for the morrow.

Rain had come into Gar's young life a year earlier when his plans to marry his beloved Kathy Doogan went awry. The record on the turntable could have been *"Stormy Weather"* with its lament that since my beloved and I have parted, it's gray rain all day long. The Irish, however, sing ballads, not "blues," to express a lost love. For Gar the Mendelssohn recording was best because it not only conveyed his sense of regret at losing the companionship of Kathy but much more it expressed the beauty of that most beautiful moment in his life—when she had joyfully agreed to be his wife.

Classical music can do that—tap our sorrow at the loss of the beloved in the same movement in which our appreciation for the beloved is reinforced beyond all telling. One March day the year after my mother had died, Karl Haas devoted one of his daily programs of classical music to the selections that were most significant in his life. My ears perked up when he played the slow movement from Beethoven's Fifth Piano Concerto. At its conclusion, Karl Haas said it was the music he had played the day he got word that his father had died. I was stunned because I had played that very same side for my mother when I had gone home to bury my dad. Mom began to cry at the music and I was about to turn it off when she said, "Oh no, please leave it on; it's beautiful and I need to let off the tears I feel." Such music relieves sorrow in plumbing our profound appreciation for the beloved who is gone. For my mother, the Beethoven passage brought back the many shining moments she had shared with my father. For Brian Friel's Gar O'Donnell, the Mendelssohn movement stood for two glowing moments—one fishing with his father, the other with Kathy Doogan planning the home they would make together.

Gar had gone home with Kathy that very same day to ask her father's permission. With a lilting word of encouragement, she had left Gar alone in the doorway to talk to her dad. But Senator Doogan did not invite him in. Instead, he intimidated Gar in relating his hopes that Kathy would marry Dr. King, the son of a classmate from University, who had just then come for dinner. Gar became tongue-tied and was made to feel inferior: his future as manager of his dad's store couldn't possibly match the "professional" circles in which the Doogans moved. Gar had left his shattered dreams on the Doogan doorstep. For whatever reasons, Gar did not have the chance to speak to Kathy again before she became Mrs. King. (Contrary to today's convenience, people in the Ireland of those days were not "as close as the telephone." Many did without—so they weren't able to keep in touch with "Touch-tone.") The interference of her father had thwarted the plans Gar and Kathy had made together. Doogan's self-willed authoritarian manner had made Gar feel so unacceptable that he simply did not have a way of keeping up courtship with Kathy. So Gar faded away without Kathy ever knowing quite why. Another breakdown in communication had frustrated Gar's yearning for belonging.

For all that the play tells us, Kathy may have been conjoined into her marriage by her socially-minded politician of a father. Doogan's misuse of parental authority is not as outmoded as it may seem: under the guise of "protecting her," fathers still obstruct their

daughter's choice of spouse or even friends—putting her in the difficult position of having to choose between father or friend. Much as
we feel for a father who realizes perhaps too late the quickness with
which his child of a daughter has become a mature woman, such over-
weening control by a parent is a violation of the trust the daughter
places in her father or mother. It is an unwarranted restriction upon
her own spontaneity in making a new home for herself with the husband of her choice. It is an attempt to manipulate her through her
natural affection for her folks. Why parents pump up their own self-
importance by exercising control over their grown children is a serial
mystery—it has been repeated throughout human history.

Senator Doogan was used to having things his own way.
Kathy's marriage to Dr. King did take place; Gar and his father had
been invited. S.B. attended, but Gar should not, could not, would not
go. Yet his thoughts were ever with Kathy. Just because she was to
marry someone else did not mean he loved her the less. He had
shared all his dreams with Kathy—even the secret of the egg-money
he made on the side that was to have helped finance their home together. Ironically, it was the day of Kathy's wedding that Aunt Lizzy
had turned up unexpectedly from America. Maybe it was the way out
Gar was looking for on that forlorn day. In any case, the visit had
ended with Gar's accepting his aunt and uncle's invitation to come
live with them in Philadelphia, where he would work as a hotel porter.

The day has now arrived for Gar to leave. Kathy comes to say
goodbye. Madge is out and S.B. is minding the store. So Gar and
Kathy have time alone together, their first since his hopeful moment
that was so soon brought low by her father. His heart is aglow at
being with Kathleen again. "Private Gar" summons the poetic lines
that symbolize total belonging for him: "It is now 16 or 17 years since
I saw the Queen of France, then the Dauphiness, at Versailles."[7] But
his very love for her keeps him from speaking his feelings. His beloved Kathleen has chosen another path in life and belongs to someone
else now. He will not burden her with any show of affection that
would put her in the predicament of regret and guilt. Oh, they do that
in the American soap operas—complicating the lives of all in reach.
Gar won't work such self-serving unkindness upon Kathy. But he
can't help being brusque with her, in hiding his disappointment that
any future for him in Ballybeg had gone dark the day of her wedding.

Kathy found Gar so unlike himself in putting down "the town he loved so well"; she couldn't fathom that Gar could not bear to say goodbye to his *mavourneen* with whom he had hoped to share home. (Kathleen Mavourneen of the old Irish song-title means "my beloved Kathleen.") It was good of her to come but the procession of their plans circled back in his consciousness as she spoke her "All the best, Gar." He'd best cut the conversation short or he'd lose his nerve about going to Philadelphia and cave in there and then.

No one leaves the home he has known except in the hopes of forming a new one. All Gar's aspirations for finding home had rested with Kathy; they had been dashed with her dad's interference. What he faced now was going to Philadelphia as an outsider with no one to share his dreams and dreads with as he had with Kathy. He wishes now he hadn't been so abrupt with her in saying goodbye because he cherishes her still in his heart of hearts. But he simply cannot get stuck at that point in his life history when he had lost his love. Such self-pity would keep him ever an outsider. What Gar comes to is full appreciation that Kathy had once loved him enough to want to share her life with him and had showered him with the affection he had never known till then. Mutuality in the total gift of friendship is a blessing so rare even in marriage that Gar is glad to have had a touch of it before he goes his lonely way to Philadelphia.

We all fear the unknown—Gar's realization that he was and in a sense still is the beloved friend of Kathy makes it easier to face the future. They had shared so much that he knows he is capable of loving and being loved and won't forever be an outsider in Philadelphia. Maybe less likely so than he would have been in the Doogans' closed circle. Gar has no illusions about Aunt Lizzy. She in her maudlin way had made him aware that she was anxious to have him in her house as the son she never had. Her gushy manner could not have been that of his mother. Gar often wondered what his mother had been like. Sometimes he would ask Madge.

All children as young adults try to capture a sense of what their parents were like when first they married. This harking back to our origins is elemental: we need to know about the persons who conceived us. To appreciate them. This is why we have to somehow settle up our relationships with our parents, no matter how late the year; no matter what frayed ends still bother us. Our parents had us and we do appreciate this—no matter what gulfs may have come between. The gap of death had made it very difficult for Gar, especially since his father rarely spoke of Maire except to remember her to God during the evening rosary. We then sense Gar's grasping for one final strand in his mother's biography when Master Boyle stops by later that afternoon to bid him adieu.

Boyle had courted his mother in times gone by. Her son had been his pupil. So the schoolmaster comes by with a book of his poetry as a going-away present. But also to ask a small loan. Boyle had remained single and his recent life had become a bout with the bottle. His latest round had put him in a fix with the local pastor. In fact, Boyle times his visit to beat the Canon's arrival for his nightly game of cards with S.B. Gar looks up at the bedraggled man who could have been his father. Boyle had once loved his mother; and his mother had chosen another path—to become the bride of S.B. O'Donnell. Had Boyle turned to drink to cover his disappointment? This notion wells up in Gar as the teacher shakes his hand, wishing him the best in America. Gar's eyes begin to water. The schoolmaster was giving Gar an advance glimpse of what could happen to him if he tumbled to his sorrow at losing his fiancée. That would be no kindness to Kathleen. Gar is grateful for Boyle's fumbling gesture in the gift of his book and senses the dire humility required of his former teacher to ask for a pound to tide him over another lonely night. Boyle was a good man, overwhelmed at not having lived the kind of life that at the heart of his being he knows, *he knows* could have been his. Besides, Gar's mother had thought a lot of him.

Then the boys show up—Ned, Tom, and Joe—all enthusiasm about what they were going to do that night. But Gar knows better. He'd grown up with them. Their braggadocio about squiring the English girls they had seen on the beach would go mute in the actual circumstance. No matter. Of such bravado are the conversations of young manhood made. In that instant Gar goes back in memory over the many evenings the four of them had walked the moonlit shore with the future as open to them as the ocean splashing upon them. The breakers had reminded them that the time for "breaking away" would come for each of them. (The foursome in the movie *Breaking Away* were from Bloomington, Indiana; but their names could have been Gar and Ned, Tom and Joe.) Each steps into the future on his own. Gar is the first to go and the boys have come to say their goodbye. Typically, it was all roistering up until that pause in camaraderie. Ned makes Gar the gift of his leather belt, shyly apologizing for his lack of a better present because of a delayed paycheck. Then the firm handshakes before the boys turn towards another night at town-center that Gar had declined. As their voices trail off in the dusk, Gar holds the moment: to treasure these moments, take in every detail, because life was good for you then—and these are good men, good people for all their frothy enthusiasm.

Gar's appreciation for their kindness had become his cushion against feeling sorry for himself. The blunt words about Ballybeg he had put to Kathy had been a clumsy attempt to cover his regrets at having to say a final adieu to her—ever! He had known a happy life in his hometown and the boys he grew up with were a good part of it. They had accepted Gar for the person he was and he never felt he had to earn their friendship. They were friends and that was it. Their sense of humor had helped him surmount the hedges of disappointment that confront every teenager growing to adulthood. Perhaps if U.S. high schools had more of this Irish touch of humor circulating in their corridors, fewer teenagers would turn to drugs or suicide attempts in their despondency at being jilted by their "steady" or failing their "finals."

Humor does relativize our setbacks—and Irish history has been so full of economic and political desperation that the people have mastered the art of humor as an antidote. First-time visitors at an Irish-American wake are sometimes taken aback at the buoyant greeting and conversation that meets them. They may not realize how often the Irish have had to face death in their family history—from the potato famine to the "troubles"; from life as fishermen in the west of Ireland to their passage to America in an infested steerage that claimed the life of a large number before arrival. (So many Irish immigrants of 1801 suffered from disease upon docking in New York that they were quarantined at Staten Island. There these Irish Catholics were attended to by Anglican-American Dr. John Bayley, the first Director of Health for the Port of New York. He was so attentive in his care that he himself succumbed to the influenza. His daughter would later carry on his work in hospitals. We know her as St. Elizabeth Bayley Seton.)

The Irish have had to live the truth of the Lord's resurrection and its promise of reunion beyond death. In their faith, not even death itself has the last word in the face of the Easter mystery of the Lord's continuing presence. Much as they carry a heavy heart at the death of the person they will bury on the morrow, the bereaved family will not lay that burden upon those who have come to pay their respects. Rather do they greet their friends and neighbors with the upbeat graciousness of a person who believes in God's caring providence.

Gar grieves for his mother a little each evening in his prayers. But humor is his characteristic way of getting beyond the disappointments he will leave behind in Ireland. The chuckle of an Irishman often masks distress. He resorts to humor amidst difficulty for two reasons: He will not visit his private anguish upon another, and since death itself is not an absolute, no other setback need be dire. This is why you will find an Irishman edgy in small matters but keeping his sense of humor in the great crises of life. No better example comes to mind than Ronald Reagan's remark right after he was shot. As he entered surgery, the President looked up at the doctors and asked, "Are you Republican or Democrat?" Nor after his return to the White House upon recovery did he ever refer to his wound again. The Irish have their faults; but humor is the restorative that keeps them from absolutizing any failure that would trap them in the ditch of self-pity. If we slip into that mudbank, we can't see beyond ourselves and will not appreciate how much love and care is actually directed our way. Gar never yielded to bitterness. He dismissed "Daddy Boy" Senator Doogan with a quip so he could focus upon his own father his final day at home.

Madge had paved the path. She was gone that afternoon to see her newborn niece who was to be named for her. The hospital visit brought different word. The baby would be baptized Brigid instead. Gar knew how much it would have meant to Madge as maiden aunt to have the infant bear her name. Madge's only comment was that Brigid Mulhern had a nice sound to it, with no hint of letdown in her voice. "Oh Madge," "private" Gar responds with his heart's meaning: "I love you more than all the rest."[8] Gar never had to measure up for Madge, who never spoke her small misery to Gar. Oh, if he got a bit fresh in his feistiness, she'd bring him down a peg. But it was Madge who had put a two-pound note in the pocket of his raincoat: a little something for the journey. Gar knew better. It was the money Madge had put aside for her foot treatment that she would now delay another month. She wouldn't be needing to be up as much to look after the boy she had raised since infancy. He was the "son"—not her own—whom she had watched become a man while her hair had turned from silky auburn to worn gray. Gar was well aware of the significance of the small wad of a bill. It meant that, given the opportunity, Madge would give everything, even life itself, for Gar. Gar knew he belonged to Madge as he did to S.B., because of their commitment of total love. Much as he appreciated the friendship of the boys, he didn't belong to them. We belong only to those who are ready to make total gift to us and we to them.

Kathy Doogan would have belonged to Gar but her father had refused to say "son" to him. Master Boyle could have conceivably said "son" to him, had Gar's mother married him. Aunt Lizzy does say "son" but it rings hollow in coming from her barrenness. Madge says "son" out of her own total devotion. She also speaks for S.B., in knowing full well that his feelings for his son run so deep that any word at all would become a stream that would keep Gar from starting his trip in the morning. My own father said little the morning he put me on the train to go far away to college—something I was reluctant to do. I still remember the marble well leading down to the train-tracks in Cleveland's Union Terminal. I wouldn't see it again for three years, when I came back home to bury my dad. I know what Gar meant when he asks Madge to let him know if anything should happen. My mother had done that sad duty for me. Gar's father had bid him goodbye with the suitcase from his honeymoon. My dad had done the same with the steamer trunk bearing his name that has kept to this day.

Brian Friel knows about good-bys. He lets "private" Gar speak the heart's meanings. S.B., however, says goodbye through gesture. Gar's dad can't sleep that last night; he comes down for tea and sags into the kitchen chair and gazes wistfully towards Gar's room. He sees the raincoat folded atop the suitcase outside the closed door. S.B. slowly gets up, goes over and touches the shoulder of the raincoat. S.B. is still warding off the chill from Gar, as he did that showery day fishing. It's his final touch of home and goodbye. The mutual appreciation of father and son is bonded in eternal communion.

- 11 -
Beginning Again

"I'M PATRICK." WHEN MY SISTER MISSED HER FIVE-YEAR-OLD FOR A moment in the dimestore, she heard his voice coming from a cluster of adults. There he was, his brown saucer-eyes scanning the arch of faces turned towards him. Patrick always drew people to him with the hint of a smile that was all gladness and trust for being with them. He could never be anyone but Patrick and never expected that anyone else would "play a role" in his presence. He was as natural as his dark curly hair that he later let grow out—Jesus-style. Providence must have favored him: just as he became president of his senior class, the high school principal put in a rule requiring boys' hair to be above the collar. His simply grew as wide as his grin, causing no problem except plugging the drain with each shampoo.

So typical of Patrick—never a man to hide behind a rule; ever a person who came clean. Racine's praise fit Patrick: *"Le ciel n'est pas plus pur que le fond de son coeur—"* "His heart was as pure as heaven itself." Maybe that's why he quit classes at the country's most prestigious school of architecture and transferred to Kent State. Academic reputations can smother spontaneity with institutional mustiness. Patrick was now finishing his degree and working part-time in a state park near Akron, Ohio. He had kept his motorcycle as an economy measure to go back and forth from his apartment to school and work. He had always wanted a "big bike," which his mother would not have on the premises because she sensed the hazard. Patrick had come to agree. Motorcycles and highway traffic don't mix. He would get rid of his as soon as he could afford a car. He played it safe Memorial Day weekend 1980 and gave up his plans to go to the Indi-

131

anapolis "500." He took a friend's place at work instead. That Saturday, he closed the park at dusk and rode back to his apartment alone. There were no witnesses to the accident. Patrick had been thrown from the motorcycle; his chin had hit the fireplug at the fork in the country road where he lay till a passerby found him. He never regained consciousness. His five sisters made sure he was buried in a plaid shirt with collar open to the wind. Patrick was a free spirit who was still so present to them. A man came to the wake who had met Patrick only once. He liked him and added, "I usually don't even talk to guys with long hair." His four brothers carried him to his grave— not near the crucifixion sculpture in Calvary cemetery but in a less expensive plot down in a hollow beneath a tree. As they reached the spot that sunny morning, his brother next in age exhaled his disbelief, "OK, Pat—you've carried this far enough." Pat had always kept things stirring, the watchspring in the family, the low-key initiator of get-togethers. No one could believe he was gone. In a sense Patrick never left because his family and friends were touched with his contagious spirit.

He had turned 22 on May 22nd. He had gone back home that day for a birthday celebration. As he blew out the candles on the cake his mom had baked, his brothers and sisters noticed how Pat had his dad's quiet way of taking everything in and his mother's bright chuckle. That was the last the family had seen him. Patrick reached eternal rest before the week was out. At graveside, his uncle read a passage from Saint Exupéry's *Pilote de guerre*, a book about a wartime mission that had taken place on Pat's birthday 40 years before. Like Pat, the aviator-author would go to his death without witnesses to his crash—but not before describing the bond that keeps a friend present beyond death: "When I lost Guillaumet, the best friend I ever had, in a plane crash, I avoided talking about him . . . We were of the same substance so that part of me died in him . . . I am one with Henri Guillaumet."[1] Pat had "squandered time" upon his parents, brothers and sisters, friends and relatives. Pat's bond with them was knit in full appreciation of being together. Their bond with Pat would keep in total gratitude for those 22 years with the 22-year-old. Pat was a "stay-at-home" after all, just as Saint Exupéry had said his venturing kind would be: "The essential is to live for the return."[2]

Patrick was also the name of Michael Finnegan's son. This Patrick never appears in the movie, *Finnegan, Begin Again*—though there's a photo of him with his father taken that last summer before he drowned at the age of 10. Nor can you simply write this Patrick off as an unreal character spoken of in a movie. Here we have to be careful of significance. Something can be real that does not exist yet, like the college graduation of your daughter next year. The event has not taken place; it doesn't exist and yet it is very real. Our goals are real—they engage our choice and give direction to our activity. On the other hand, there may actually be a boy in the U.S. somewhere named Patrick Finnegan with a father named Michael. But you've never heard of them so their existence is of no significance to you. It is a matter of fact, not of value. It is not real for you. This is not to confuse life depicted in a movie with factual existence. Yet the truths and values that Robert Preston as Michael Finnegan communicates about his relationship with his son Patrick are as real and significant for our own living as the biographical account of Charles de Gaulle's tender relationship with his retarded daughter, Anne.

Starting with *The Music Man*, Robert Preston was incapable of being unreal in any movie or play he appeared in. He himself had remarked that trying out for the lead in Meredith Willson's wonderful piece of Americana was like Caruso singing "*O Solo Mio.*" Even Preston's parlance tumbles with life. *Finnegan, Begin Again* carries that touch of extra urgency that W.B. Yeats speaks of "when the singer began to sing into the rocking cradle or among the winecups and it was though life itself caught fire of a sudden."[3] Perhaps Preston sensed that this was to be his final movie. He tells of his last long conversation with son Patrick Finnegan in as real a way as my sister did of hers with son Patrick Brett. It's Yeats again who claims that the arts are the spear whose handle is our daily life. I must say that the movie came through to me and helped me get a handle on the meaning of relationship with a nephew who died all too young. The Gospels give solace, but maybe our best movies serve like the pictorial commentary we find in the church art of the Gothic age. Cathedrals like Strasbourg and Chartres braid images of everyday life into the great scenes from Jesus' life. They have no sound track; but the poesie and song of bards like Wolfram von Eschenbach dubbed in the meanings suggested by the sculptures, carvings and stained glass.

Not that the ditty Michael Finnegan would sing to his son was a song of the bard or even the lullaby Yeats refers to. It was simply a little verse to which Michael could skip a bit of a jig to the delight of wife and son:

> There was an old man named Michael Finnegan.
> He grew whiskers on his chin again;
> He shaved them off but they grew in again.
> Poor old Michael Finnegan, Begin again!

Michael repeated the song the day his son said he wished their summer would never end. After his son had been taken from him, that summer never did. But Michael himself had to begin again. The mysteries of death and other human failing have to be confronted if we are going to get on with life. If we avoid the issue, we'll always be a restless son on the run, never having the hope and the trust to become a homebody again. Instead we'll try to be somebody or a busybody but this will keep us on edge and never let us get back home to stay— to nest or rest, emotionally speaking, on the welcoming shoulder of our beloved.

Michael Finnegan had become a stay-at-home after an extramarital affair. Not a fling exactly. He loved the girl, though they were together only four months. It ended, as he acknowledges, in the quickest way known to man: his wife found out. Michael was not guilt-ridden because he had never stopped loving his wife. But he deeply regretted having hurt her. She forgives him his infidelity and Michael Finnegan begins again. There's happiness again in home life as Patrick grows into boyhood. A decade of family that never would have been theirs if his wife had refused to forgive. Maybe that's why Jesus merges our request for daily bread in the Lord's prayer with the give and take of forgiveness. Our bread is belonging whose leaven is mutual listening, acceptance, and forgiveness. Without forgiveness, Michael and his wife would never have known one another well enough again to raise Patrick. Without forgiveness, Michael would never have become a stay-at-home. Without forgiveness, Michael would never have accepted himself and would ever be trying to win back his wife's love. And they would never have known what it is to miss a son.

The continuing mystery in human relations still centers in marriage. If a husband has sexual relations with his secretary whom he has come to love as a good friend, does that mean he no longer loves his wife? We would be inclined to say no, wouldn't we, though we would also say that it does great hurt to the wife. But how does it do such hurt? By being excluded from that dimension of her husband's life that belongs to her. But what do we mean by that? We don't really want to reduce their marital union simply to going to bed together and "making love." Otherwise, we would practically be saying it's all right for the husband to love his secretary—to the exclusion of his wife—so long as he doesn't go to bed with her. According to this scenario, he could be sharing his heart and all his being with his secretary and coming home and being very reserved with his wife, even in going to bed with her. Sexual intimacy is not the barometer of good communication in marriage. Why, then, should a marriage break down completely because a husband has sexual relations with a woman who is a good friend of his?

I've run through this little litany of inconsistency to show how we really do narrow the meaning of marital fidelity to monagamous sexual relations. Pyschologists report, however, that when a husband has an affair, the motivation is more often emotional need for personal "space" than sexual gratification. Consequently, it is part of the wisdom Anne Lindbergh relates to be keenly aware of a spouse's yearning for his or her own space; over-possessiveness in whatever guise will have a spouse "wanting out." Furthermore, the understanding that leads to forgiveness transcends the notion of adultery which concentrates solely on sexual intimacy; true compassion attends to the personal need of the spouse for acceptance just as he or she is. One form of marital claustrophobia that is nearly intolerable is setting up expectancy levels that are so unrealistic that a spouse knows he or she can never live up to them. In such a situation many a spouse will seek relief in some sort of escape, though this will not further his or her sense of self-acceptance.

Self-acceptance. It goes back to the mother-child relationship in which the infant first became conscious of itself as a distinctive human being. John Bannister Tabb put this home truth in brief verse:

> The baby has no skys
> But mother's eyes;
> Nor any God above
> But mother love;

His angel sees the Father's face
But he, the mother's full of grace.
And yet of such as this
The heavn'ly kingdom is![4]

Self-acceptance is registered in his or her bitty being in the glowing countenance of mother and dad looking down upon him. The poet-prophet Hosea, in fact, pictures God's communication of his love to us as grace with the image of God leaning over the cradle and bringing the infant up to the shoulder of his embrace. Things go swimmingly for the child until that day near two-years-old when he or she waxes independent and sweeps the tiny jar of Beechnut Baby Food from the tray of his high chair, as if to say "Make mine Gerber's." In that instant, his ears immediately resound with two back-to-back claps: that of the jar hitting the kitchen floor and his mother's palm boxing his ear. The child's in tears—stunned, nonplussed, looking up to that once loving face that is now a thundercloud, as if to plead, "Where did it all go wrong, Mom?" His world has now tilted away from the warmth of love to the chill of isolation in which the child first comes to doubt his self-acceptance.

It's good to remember that our self-acceptance didn't start with self but with the gracious regard of our parents or those who raised us in infancy in place of parents. It is the primary relationship; psychologists "instinctively" (I like that) go back to that beginning and early threats to it to get a read on a patient's hangups. One day I watched such a scene unfold between mother and five-year-old daughter on a Strasbourg street. The mother had become miffed with the child for whatever reason. The girl then started to cry and wouldn't follow along. With that the mother walked on alone while the child hid in the doorway of a store. The mother looked back and detected a telltale scarf so she kept on her way. The daughter would not have her mother get too far ahead so she skipped to another doorway a few yards along. The mother would not let the child have her stubborn way nor would the child let the mother out of her sight. Her self-acceptance was too tied into her mother, in spite of her fledgling attempts to take wing on her own as an independent person. Our sense of self-acceptance started in our consciousness of being worthy of the love of our parents. When that love is removed, however temporarily, doubt about our worth and self-acceptance intrudes, so we turn elsewhere to recover it. But there is no one else. So, now we have to earn back our parents' love by doing what they tell us and living up to their expectations. Our worth and self-acceptance have now become tied to conduct and performance of tasks.

But Mom and Dad did provide an "out"—in instilling through night prayers the belief that God is a Father who loves us always and that his son Jesus, who's human like us, died for our sins. Sin? What's that? Oh, that's hurting God. How do we hurt God? The nun in second grade preparing us for First Communion says that disobeying our parents is a sin. So God backs up my parents; now I've got to earn his love too. Besides, if I commit adultery—that's a mortal sin that puts me in hell forever unless I go to confession to the priest. In fact, before I can make my First Communion, I'll be eight in May, I've got to clear all these sins from my soul by making my first confession. I have to make sure I'm in God's good graces because going to communion in the state of "mortal sin" would be another "mortal sin." Wow—ee. Can't even God who knows me better than anybody love me as I am?

This, of course, is a parody of what we know of God's love for us as revealed in Jesus. But, sorry to say, the caricature was the catechesis presented to many of us who grew up in the Roman Church before the Second Vatican Council. That notion of God was so contrary even to the Old Testament God of Hosea who did not turn his back on Israel in its sinfulness precisely because Israel was his child. And Jesus' portrait of God as the father of the prodigal son carried no judgmental anger at all. It is the son who had turned away! The father misses him so—and looks down the road each day to see if he might be coming home. In fact, it is the unconditional love of the Father that gives the wayward boy the abiding sense of self-worth, in spite of messing up, that has him trust that his father will take him back. There it is in a nutshell. Self-acceptance rests in the trust a person has that another will take him just as he or she is, for interior worth rather than exterior accomplishment or measuring up to some level of expectancy. We're not talking Olympics. You don't have to bring home a medal, no matter what the CBS commentator might intimate. All the prodigal son brought home was his trust that the father would welcome him home. Somehow the father had gotten across to that son the notion his elder brother had failed to fathom: "Son, you are always with me and everything I have is yours." (Lk. 15:31) The father Jesus depicts as God was not into performance ratings so his son didn't have to measure up because he always had worth as the beloved of the father from the very start. The son had obviously come to that interior sense of self-acceptance in the time father and son had "squandered together," who knows how. Maybe looking all the way to snow-capped Mt. Hermon from the Galilee hills in Jay and Rufus fashion or fishing on Lake Kinnaret like Gar and S.B. O'Donnell. (We *squander time* with God in prayer).

Kinnaret is Hebrew for "harp" (the shape of the lake Jesus knew), so it fits the Irish setting of Brian Friel's reverie of father and son spending time together. This is a favorite passage of mine and I included it in a talk I once gave to a Long Island church group. A man came up to me afterwards with tears in his eyes. He said he was going to take his son fishing that very next Saturday. With lots of repeats. The tears had come from unhappy memories of his own boyhood weekends. He had worked for his father who owned a tavern. The sad refrain that still pounded in his ears was "Bring up another case of beer, you son of a b. . . ." The unfeeling parent never interspersed a word of thanks, much less affection, with his phony macho talk. The boy never had experienced a moment when his father showed appreciation for him to give his boy some sense of self-worth. The father never had time for him, yet expected his young son to do a man's work. This good youngster now grown to adulthood and a father himself had already broken the cycle of verbal violence in his respect for his son. He realized the importance of spending profitless time with his son, waiting for the fish to bite. They could be alone together in full appreciation of what a rare privilege it is to acknowledge one another's worth. The son did not have to meet a quota of stacked beer cases as the criterion for acceptance. A curious thing had happened. The father could accept himself in receiving the appreciation from his son that he had never experienced from his own father.

Every son looks up to his father and yearns for his father's approval. Without it, the boy is under relentless pressure to prove himself in order to find some sense of interior worth and self-acceptance. This was the shadow over Cal's existence as we meet him in the movie version of John Steinbeck's *East of Eden*. Raymond Massey played the role of single parent to Aaron and Caleb with the Bible reading righteousness of an unbending prairie patriarch. Except that his farm was in the lettuce-growing Sacramento valley. The older boy Aaron was the father's favorite who could do no wrong; the younger son Cal could never seem to do anything right. He was practically an orphan—the mother was a "wayward woman" who had scampered out of the rigid household and stayed out of sight. So Cal desperately needed to do something to win his father's love. Cal, so sensitively played by James Dean to Julie Harris' Kathy, engages the help of Kathy to set up a way of making a profit on the farm produce. But, because Cal's enterprise outdid that of the local growers, his hard work brought only his father's displeasure. Cal's earnings were to have been his surprise birthday present for his father. And the father turned it aside—along with Cal's hopes for self-acceptance. In a subtle swing of focus, we come to realize that the father's stern attitude towards Cal harks back to the failure he feels for his wife's having left him. His inflexible stance towards her had cost him his marriage and had made him cover the failings of which he was so conscious in himself.

Acknowledgement of failings within oneself begins with forgiveness of failings in another. This wisdom, going back to Jesus, is that if I can forgive the faults that bother me in a friend, then maybe I can begin to believe that she will forgive the inadequacies I am so conscious of in myself and which I have forever tried to cover, to keep winning her approval and friendship. Gibson Winter, in his book, *Love and Conflict*, sheds light on this hidden benefit of forgiveness:

> He now begins to reveal himself to her as he really is. Some of the pretense slips away. The relationship takes on some reality. He begins to find a capacity to accept himself through his acceptance of her. He can live with himself without pretending because he can live with her without making her into someone else.[5]

Forgiveness in accepting a spouse as she is becomes the key to self-acceptance. In Michael and Margaret Finnegan's situation, this led to a mutual decision to stay together in marriage. But for many a couple this forgiveness and reciprocal self-acceptance may lead to a discovery: that they aren't friends after all and never were. They had been very friendly, enjoyed each other's company and got on together very well. They had married on the basis of certain qualities each had found attractive in the other. But after the honeymoon and settling down to the routine of household living, she discovers that her husband hadn't married a wife at all but a mother-substitute. Someone that will put up with his drinking or going out with "the boys" as a perpetual college undergraduate—or with his mean streak! There's the rub: a mother can never totally disown a child because he or she belongs to her in an undeniable sense. But it is not the same with friendship, even married friendship. The bond of friendship cannot withstand assaults upon friendship itself. A child, to cite a tragic instance, may put up with violence coming from a parent because the relationship is inescapable. But violence shown a friend devastates the relationship there and then.

Friendship is based on mutual respect; the show of violence not only sullies this respect but introduces the fear of physical harm that undermines the bond of friendship. A wife can forgive her husband's sexual infidelity that was prompted by the motive of love—hurtful as her sense of rejection may have been in that instance. But a wife cannot remain the sincere friend of a husband whose violence has made her afraid. A woman cannot truthfully love a man who has made her fear for her life. For all her attachment to him for his engaging qualities, down deep she trembles. Friendship cannot survive such self-protective fear because the core of friendship is *mutual* respect and affection creating peace and trust.

If the wife stays with a husband who has physically threatened her, the marriage becomes a defensive alliance maintained for economic reasons or "for the children's sake." Neither consideration is good enough. Acknowledging the failings of the husband in this dire context is also to admit that the marriage is faltering. It may be that the best forgiveness in his regard is separation and divorce. Perhaps this would give the husband a chance at changing his ways and to begin again with a new friend. But it would be pseudo-acceptance of the husband to gloss over the violence that has already invaded the home. His can no longer be a welcoming shoulder because his violence has made her ever fearful for herself in his presence. Wives who stay with such misfitting husbands do so as mothers covering for a troubled child or as nurses treating a psychotic patient. But such "martyrdom" has no place in friendship. Furthermore, the children of a marriage deserve peace in their homelife coming from parents who respect and love one another as friends and equals. Fortunately, current employment opportunities in the U.S. make it possible for a woman to face the prospect of becoming a single parent with a viable income. Economic reasons cannot be allowed to trap a person in a relationship that has become intolerable. Facing up to this violent streak in a spouse is not easy for a wife who has been so deft in keeping his dark side from the neighbors. It is even difficult to bring up in this discussion of acknowledging the failings in the spouse and in oneself. But no one really accepts violence as part of marriage or any friendship. There is so much terror in the world—hardly a day goes by without TV reporting another incident—that our homes must remain a haven of peace.

Such peace comes when each spouse can be true to himself or herself in admitting what each has been seeking in marriage. If it has been anything other than friendship, including the bond with the children, then separation is the honest path because friendship, especially married friendship, knows no hidden agenda. John Macmurray won't let us forget this fundamental truth: "If the relationship had any other reason for it, we should say that one or other of them was pretending friendship from an ulterior motive. This means in effect that friendship is a type of relationship into which persons enter with the whole of themselves."[6]

If a person lets career, business or individual advancement take precedence over this primary gift to spouse or friend, he or she is no longer *being* friend to the other, however much this may be layered over with long hours of household work and hovering attention. Can't play games here; too much is at stake. It will be easier to let the truth emerge if we can clear away faulty assumptions at the outset. First, there is no inherent evil in putting career or business success ahead of married friendship; it frankly means that this friendship has succumbed in the thicket of those other concerns Jesus speaks of in his parable of the sower. Secondly, there is no such thing as a marriage that failed. If there were a marriage at all, there was a total exchange of the personal self-gift that forms the union of friendship. Such a union has an "eternal" dimension whose value keeps as a golden moment in one's living. An authentic marriage can never have been a failure; it was a marriage that didn't last.

Of course, many a couple go down the aisle after repeating their nuptial vows who never make total gift to one another. They are legally married but there never was a marriage or even a friendship there. Just a mutually suitable partnership which each entered with ulterior motives, whether of comfortable lifestyle or reliable service from the other. A congenial couple, really. Congeniality, however, is a sign of friendliness, not friendship. Jules Toner, in his much-too-neglected book, *The Experience of Love,* goes right to the core of friendship to tell the difference in careful language:

> The giving which is love is not merely a giving *to* someone for the other to possess and use. The giving which is an act of radical love is a giving *into,* so that by it the gift is *in* the loved. Neither is it a giving into someone a gift other than self as a symbol of self and his love. It is not even a giving into the beloved something *of* self. It is a giving *self;* for it is myself who am in the loved one by my love, not merely my possessions or even my thoughts, my wit, my joy, my wisdom, my strength. It is myself.[7]

Better read the paragraph over again; my old colleague, Jules, makes his philosopher distinctions that are the key to understanding. (Thirty years ago, his University of Detroit students would give Fr. Toner a standing ovation at the end of his course on "Love." Here we have a hint of why; he took his subject much too seriously to resort to the stroking or sloganeering that mar so many self-help books on the subject.) John Macmurray had anticipated Jules' analysis with his own description of personal realization through spontaneous self-donation to another: "Self-expression is the expression of that capacity to enter into the life of the other and to be absorbed in it . . ."[8]

The mutual self-giving that marks authentic friendship and marriage is almost mute, as my mentor, Robert Johann, hymns in his own book on love:

> One of love's most curious paradoxes is what we may call its reticence. The deeper the love, the less it has to say in its own defense. Its sincerity can almost be measured by its speechlessness. Its very directness imposes silence. When love is interested, when the attraction is based on a motive of profit or need, it has no difficulty in finding words to justify itself. When "I love you" equals "I want you," the expected satisfac-

tion of the want is reason enough for the love. You are clever, and so you can solve my doubts; you are rich, and so you can pay my debts; you are physically beautiful, and so you can satisfy my passion; or even, you are virtuous, and so you can teach me goodness. In short, you are such and such, and so I love you. But what about the love that is tongue-tied? What about the love that is only sure of itself but cannot give a "why or wherefore?" Why do I love you? Because you are—*You.* That is the best it can do. It is indefensible . . . Yet all the world pays it homage. The other type of love is technically only desire.[9]

The three philosophers, Macmurray, Toner and Johann insist that married friendship cannot survive the dominant desire for individual accomplishment that pushes aside other considerations. It is not surprising, therefore, that the bicentennial rise of the "yuppies" with their "dinc" (double income, no children) marriages was matched with an increase in divorce. A decade later, Lady Liberty would celebrate her own centennial with the co-op apartments of yuppiedom now lining the Hudson. Her "tired and poor" had been shoved out by the pile-drivers of the "me" generation. But the wise "lady" was not fooled, for all the fireworks. These plush buildings could not be symbols of progress if the divorce rate in the area had reached 50%. Something drastic had occurred: divorce had soared because spouses had changed.

People *do* change. That's the hardest truth to face in friendship and in marriage. Anne Lindbergh had reassured us that the forms of friendship and marriage would not stay the same. But what about the spouse? Cannot he or she remain the good and loving person I married? Of course, unless other values come to be more important in his or her living—like the pull of one's profession. Jim Palmer talked about that. He had been a professional baseball pitcher, but he quit with the goal of 300 major league victories within reach. Why? His two teenaged daughters wanted him to go for it. But Jim refused. His reason: he wanted to spend time with these daughters before they left home; baseball had already deprived him of the chance of watching them grow up. Jim was direct: "If he had spent as much time on his family as he did on baseball, he would still be married." Once I asked a student whose own parents were divorced what was more important: saving your job or keeping a friend. She answered without hesitancy:

"Keeping the friend because you'll have her long after you've changed jobs." No wonder Anne Lindbergh gives us an advance glimpse of middle-age when we will drop the masks of ambition and pride anyway if we have learned anything at all from life. If we fathom these truths early, we'll still have friends to invite into our shell, those sincere friends who make home a haven of peace. Jim Palmer took up a second career as a sports commentator. This gave him a chance to see his two best friends often during the week . . . his two daughters.

Careers can be balanced with dedication to family and friends if we keep our values straight. Richard Daly, Sr. did. He grew up at 35th and Wabash, went to de la Salle Institute on the corner, got his business degree at night and became one of Chicago's best mayors—Mike Royko's book, *Boss*, notwithstanding. But his focus was always upon his wife and his seven children. He never left the neighborhood, but looked forward to summer vacation with Sis and the kids at the old Foote cottage in Grand Beach, Michigan. Three incidents come to mind from Richard Daly's life that reveal his integrity. The first was just about that—as he confided to a reporter: "I never took a dishonest dime in my life; if I had, you would have known about it by now." Then there was his touching defense of his son's engagement to the daughter of Tony Arcardo, the reputed head of the local crime syndicate. Dick Daly told the press: "My son is engaged to a lovely young woman whom he met completely on his own. They became close friends on their own. What her father does for a living and what his father does for a living have nothing to do with their friendship and marriage. So please do them the courtesy of letting them prepare for this wonderful event in their lives the way you would want it for your own sons and daughters."

The last event came on a December evening shortly before his death. Dick Daly went over to the Jesuit high school on Roosevelt Road to dedicate a gymnasium. His youngest son had gone there to school; and his second-oldest daughter, Mary Carol, had attended dances there—in an old Army Quonset hut of a gym. Dick Daly was keen to such things. So when he noticed a small parcel of land next to the school in the urban renewal plans for the area, he made it available to St. Ignatius. He had gone over to accept the Jesuits' thanks, a week before Jesus offered his. I add mine now because it was my band, "The Melody Knights," that played those dances in that Quonset hut.

(It wasn't "The Blue Note" on Dearborn Street; but my tenor saxophonist, who now teaches ethics at Loyola University as Jesuit Father Philip Grib, is still the best side-man around town.)

Richard Daly was another stay-at-home. His heart belonged to Sis and the children; being mayor was the job he did in the Loop. He helped Chicago remain a friendly big city because it was home to him. Also because Dick Daly always listened to Sis. His wife knew he wasn't perfect and he didn't have to be. He had nothing to hide from Sis so he could pay attention to her.

Self-acceptance and forgiveness free a person to listen to another. Really listen. Listening begins when a person is no longer concerned with self, either to insist upon his or her worth or to cover up a fault. Most of us hear what the other person is saying; but how often we miss hearing her meanings. We have set up expectancies in our attitude towards our spouse or friend that filter out any discourse that doesn't cue to those aspirations.

There's another French maxim that says "To understand everything about your friend is to forgive everything about him." Even his not listening! So, when your friend says to you, "I tried to tell you but you wouldn't listen," she's really forgiving you. Now you can listen. To what? What her real yearnings are in the relationship—and the anxiousness. Like what? Well, did you ever stop to think that maybe you don't have to ply her with gifts? She prefers your presence to presents. She may feel uneasy because this puts her "under obligation" and she likes to keep things simple.

Listening commences when I no longer depend upon my beloved to fill up my loneliness and to pump up my sense of significance. For expecting this of the beloved becomes almost a demand which is no longer the affirmation of the friend but desire for comfort or reassurance in oneself. Listening is a good sign of the radical love that Jules Toner defines as "co-being the beloved." Listening is unencumbered by the lumber of preconceived notions or laws that can keep a friend from speaking what's on her mind. The heart has its meanings that are priceless because their source is that unique person who thought enough of me to become my friend. The loneliest gaps in a relationship come about when I've blocked her ability to be open with me because she's afraid she'll hurt me or shock me because of my inflexible outlook on life. How easy it is to frame a friend in our preset categories of expectancy. We often see in another, even our closest associate, what we want to see; we hear only what we want to hear. How difficult it is to free ourselves from our background to appreciate the person who is really there before me—as Sydney Harris reminds us:

> We enter a restaurant, and six persons are sitting there. What do we "see" beyond the mere fact that these are six human beings? Do we see the same picture, either individually or collectively? A European will note that these are six Americans, by their dress and attitudes. A woman entering the room will probably note that the six consist of two married couples, an older woman, and a single man. A Southerner will see one man who could possibly be a light-skinned Negro. A homosexual will single out one of the men as a fellow gay. An anti-Semite will immediately label one of the couples as "Jewish" A salesman will divide the group into "prospects" and "duds." And the waiter, of course, does not see people at all, but a "station" and "food" and "drinks." . . . Each of us perceives what our past has prepared us to perceive: we select and distinguish, we focus on some objects and relationships, and we blur others, we distort objective reality to make it conform to our needs or hopes or fears or hates or envies or affections . . . Our very act of seeing is warped by what we have been taught to believe, by what we want to believe, by what (in a deeper sense) we need to believe. And this is the main reason that communication is so difficult![10]

What Sydney Harris says about our perception of others can also apply to our listening—but with a caution: we can tune people out of our hearing without their ever suspecting. We can nod approval or look interested in what they are saying while our "private" self has already switched off any listening. What is the sensor that does that? Sydney Harris provides some hints from the way we censor our perceptions; but John Macmurray perhaps provides the best clues for our not listening: We don't want to hear anything that will disillusion us or cause pain. We have our own cherished image of our best friend: so when she starts saying nasty things to me, I tune her out because my own sense of well-being was built on her positive and encouraging words, not these cutting remarks that disturb my aplomb. I had built my nest of self-assurance on the feathers of her compliments, not on the homely straw of honest self-appraisal. Yet, if I let her candid talk "take," and start listening to her and the *cri de coeur* that has triggered her salvos, I will soon realize that she loves me amidst my straw. Disillusionment is the paving stone of a lasting friendship, if ever there were a friendship there. The most distressing message we ever want to hear is that our friend no longer loves us, so we put off the disillusionment by hanging up the receiver of interior listening. But then the relationship is permanently "off the hook."

Listening can hurt; and we don't like to experience hurt, especially from the person who means most to us. This is John Macmurray's best insight into why we don't listen—we don't want to hear anything unpleasant, especially if it should upset our cherished impressions about ourselves in the eyes of others. Macmurray, however, suggests that unless a person is willing to suffer unpleasant experience, he or she will never come to know the beauty and interior worth of another.[11] A person who tunes out the pain of a friend is no friend at all. Yet a person who has galvanized himself or herself against discomfort or pain has already blocked his capacity for listening to another. To listen to another presumes a readiness and a willingness to share his or her pain. Michael Finnegan was ready and willing to listen to his wife's pain.

After Patrick died, Michael's wife had retreated into a fantasy world where she imaged herself the dancer she once was. Michael, however, did not fade away, though he had to make do with the slovenly house he came home to. Her drinking didn't help. But Michael was still understanding, though once in his dismay he called out, "Margaret, where are you—ever?" He had just been mugged on his doorstep and was needing her help with some analgesic. He didn't get upset—he felt the loss of Patrick too. And if she got off her suspicious reply when he phoned to say he would be late coming home from work, he could take that too. The hurt of his early affair had left its scar. Besides, Margaret had reason—Michael would be late because he was going to supper with a divorcée he had gotten to know in a laundromat. She had come by his newspaper office because somehow he knew all about her.

Elizabeth thought him a clairvoyant, but Michael explains that he had simply combined tell-tale signs of her unhappy love affair. For all his upbeat, Preston-style talk, Michael listened with his eyes and let his gentle voice be the caressing glance of welcome. His words were always compassionate, never wry or sly, so you didn't really have to look his way to know you belonged in his company. He didn't buy the corporate canard that strong men look the other straight in the eye in the way of Wyatt Earp. No, he wasn't into that kind of eyeball wrestling. (What if you lost your contact lenses?) Maybe he had read that old *hildalgo* Ignatius Loyola's primer on good manners that advises against staring a person down. Jesus himself had doodled in the dust of the Temple courtyard rather than confront the adulteress with his gaze. He looked up only after he had spoken the reassurance that restored her dignity as a person. No, the eyes can listen because they are silent and can read the interior distress for which the other may lack the words to address. Besides, if I'm reticent with my eyes, that gives you a chance to wrap me in your own regard, to create the trust you need to open up with me. You know, the way children do; the way we all do. People who are shy with their eyes invite the confidence that an imposing stare would put off. Think how often your closest friend looks away, if only to keep spontaneity in conversation or to verify Saint Exupéry's wonderful insight: "Love is not gazing at each other—it is looking at the world over each other's shoulder."[12]

Michael's dinner with Elizabeth had reinstilled her sense of self-acceptance that had been sorely damaged, first by her divorce and now by her lover Paul's refusal to marry her because of his children. (How often it happens that men favor their offspring ahead of the woman with whom they are having an affair. So much for undying devotion!) Michael told Liz the truth with candid sincerity—but with the voice of tenderness. Furthermore, he was not visiting upon Liz any personal dread of loneliness, much as he enjoyed her company. He was "Begin again," Finnegan—Michael realized that the future is all that is open to any of us and towards which we walk with full stride in the confidence of golden moments from our past. But Michael did not try to make up for the past; that would have been an unwise weight upon the future. Nor did he try to retrieve the wonderful conversations he had had with Margaret before Patrick's drowning had enshrouded her. What he could do and did was to rekindle the motives that had first brought them together as best friends. He did this after he had taken her to the hospital—she had suffered a stroke when she had come upon burglars ransacking their house. But Michael almost didn't make it back for hospital visits. The loss of Patrick and now Margaret's stroke had darkened his existence so much that he sat unshaven amidst the shambles the robbers had made of the home he had once known. The motives to begin again were damped down to a flicker. Except that Elizabeth now listened with her eyes. She came by to check on the friend who had been so gracious in listening to her own heart's ache.

It's now her voice that does the welcoming as she invites Michael to her apartment where she cooks dinner for him. He is himself again as he spells daily visits to see Margaret with clearing out the house with Liz's help. His spirits are now riding so high that he instills new life in Margaret, whose chances for recovery have improved. He does his little jig at the foot of her hospital bed that brings the first chuckle he's heard from her in months. She gathers her breath enough to say, "I love you, Michael." She hadn't said that to him in years. No, he hadn't tried to recover the past when he would hear those words every night during their courtship. But Margaret was making a new start too. And Michael was rebounding. Elizabeth muses in disbelief, "I think you lied about your age." He responds in a line tailored for Robert Preston: "Oh, inside I'm 20; maybe 22!" He is planning Margaret's return home when the phone rings. His wife's condition had taken a sudden turn and she was dead. Silence. A time for listening with the heart. Nothing to do but begin again.

Elizabeth comes over after the funeral. She has made the final break with Paul. So Michael feels she's ready for his question, "When are you going to stop latching on to these klutzes and find somebody who will love you for yourself?" "Like whom?" "Like me!" Liz's eyes are moons of surprise: "Well, why didn't you say so in the first place?" (The scene suits Mary Tyler Moore's Liz to a T.) Michael is sincere and honest—"Now wait, I'm O.K. now, but in 10 years it's a toss-up." Now it's her voice that enfolds him in her welcoming glance: "I'd be glad to have 10 wonderful years in exchange for the 40 indifferent ones I've had." Michael and Liz begin again together in mutual self-acceptance, forgiveness and listening. She is so much Michael now that she shares his grief for Margaret and joins him in his youthful summer with Patrick that will never end. Life is like that between two good friends. Robert Preston's Michael is "a late October rose"—to borrow his line from the musical, *I Do, I Do*—that will bloom and bloom and bloom. Because he has his Elizabeth as his rose who had let him "squander time" upon her in the garden of her heart.

- 12 -

Flying Home

ANTOINE MARIE-ROGER DE SAINT EXUPÉRY LIVED HIS TRUTH TO THE finish. Until he fell from the sky on a perfectly clear day, July 31st, 1944. Nobody knows how. The log entry simply reads: "Pilot did not return." But Saint Exupéry had kept to his interior covenant—to be a participant in freeing France from Nazi tyranny. He couldn't languish on the sidelines while his comrades, along with young Americans and other Allies, poured out their life's blood for his homeland. Antoine would do it "his way," though—unarmed in a P-38 reconnaissance plane. His peace—above the swirl of "superpatriot" French factionalism, pumped-up propaganda, and hollow wartime bravado—came "in soaring for hours over France all alone in a single-seat plane shooting photos."[1] That final morning he had been taking pictures of his birthplace over Lyons and his sister Didi's town on the Côte d'Azur. In a real sense, Saint Exupéry was "flying home" when the end came.

He had written his cousin back in February that friendship, house and garden were the only values that meant anything to him. These were "home" for him. Nothing else mattered to him except the actions that would create the context of home. On the eve of his last flight, he wrote his "truth" to his best friend: "Virtue is saving the spiritual heritage of France as curator of the library at Carpentras; it is flying in an unarmed airplane; it is teaching a child how to read; it is being ready to die in working one's craft."[2] This wasn't empty rhetoric, we know, because Saint Exupéry said little and acted much. His way of putting it is precise: "You are revealed in your action: this is your true identity."[3] His books were his contribution to the tradition of his homeland—as spiritual as any to be published in our time. He participated

150

in the liberation of his country in as nonmilitant a way as he knew—taking reconnaissance photos in an unarmed airplane. And he died doing his job—probably because problems with his engine or oxygen supply forced him down to a lower altitude where his plane became an easy target for German *Messerschmitts.* He had almost been shot down by one of these fighter planes "at the very hour," as he put it, "when I turned 44."[4] That was back on June 29th.

Providence, however, was saving Saint Exupéry for one more celebration before he packed it in: to be the godfather of Christian Antoine Gavoille, his commandant's son. The only joyful lines we read in all his correspondence in that last year of his war-weary life was his telegram to the proud mother: "Heartiest congratulations on the birth of my godson who will have the kindest godfather in all this world . . . see you soon."[5] He flew over to Tunis for the baptism that took place on July 24th. How it warmed Antoine's heart to have a namesake. Young Chris was the child he would have taught to read—Saint Exupéry had written his own mother that his happiest memories were of his childhood and Christmas candles. But God took him a week later on the feast of Ignatius Loyola, the soldier saint. Christian Gavoille is nearly 50 now, and in a profound sense he still has the most compassionate godfather a child could ever have. Uncle Antoine never had the chance to teach him to read but he left behind books which burst with affection and appreciation for all those who touched Saint Exupéry's heart. Christian Antoine Gavoille was a touch of "home" for Saint Exupéry as he lifted the infant to his shoulder in welcoming love. Providence had given Antoine de Saint Exupéry, who had lost his own father at the age of four, one final moment of communion before his plane went down in "the bay of Angels."

Flying home was the longing of Antoine's heart. In his last letter to his mother, which reached her a full year after he was lost in action, the pilot poured out his yearnings: "Oh, when will I be able to tell those I love how much I do?"[6] Like hundreds of thousands who succumbed during the war, Saint Exupéry never saw his beloved again. Nor was he able to speak his affection for them in person. Yet, years later, President Charles DeGaulle would write his mother to assure her that her "son is living among us still." The last three books to come out in his lifetime became Saint Exupéry's enduring way of saying to all those near his heart, from his aging mother to new-born Christian Gavoille, how much they meant to him.

It is now 50 years since Antoine de Saint Exupéry published *Pilote de guerre* (*Flight to Arras*), *Lettre à un otage* (*Letter to a Hostage*), and *Le Petit Prince* (*The Little Prince*). He had written them during his exile in the U.S. where he had embarked after the fall of France. The one long book, *Pilote de guerre,* describes a reconnaissance mission Saint Exupéry flew over Arras during the hopeless battle of France in the spring of 1940. The book is a tribute to his comrades in group 2/33, but much more than that. Antoine weaves into his text grateful allusions to the young person for whom he was ready to give his life: the niece of the farmer with whom he stayed. He belonged to her because he had risked his life for her—he says so: "I returned from my mission over Arras, having formed my bond with my farmer's niece. Her smile became the crystal in which I could see my village and beyond my village, my homeland and beyond France all other nations."[7] It was the smile of the niece that had made him feel at home in the farmer's family: "She lifted her eyes towards me with a hint of a smile . . . This touched me in a profound way, making me feel I belonged here and no place else!"[8] That young girl would be in her 60s now, but through all these decades past she has had those lovely lines folded into his book that are for her only. This was Saint Exupéry's way of telling one certain person he loved how much he did. Antoine had solved the perennial puzzle that confronts every man in love: Like the steelworker who painted "I love you, Irene" on the top girder of a New York construction project, he wants to tell the whole world how special his beloved is to him. Yet, the same shy quality that endears her to him keeps a sensitive person like Saint Exupéry from embarrassing her with public attention. He has made all of us who read his book aware of how much she meant to him, and still protected her privacy so that she, she alone has his book as no one else does.

"You, yourself, will have the stars as no one else does"[9] are, in fact, the words of friendship that Antoine has the little prince speak in his best-known work. He dedicates *Le Petit Prince* to a specific friend, Leon Woerth—upfront. This leaves the book itself, so small and yet so universal in its appeal and symbolism, free for each of his friends to fill in the meanings. He set down this primer of personal values in the form of a children's story so no adult could mistake his point. (One of the ironies is that many an adult misses the chance to read *The Little Prince* because bookstore people stack it as a children's story—which it is not. Children are naturally baffled by his reflections upon experiences they could not yet have had.) Antoine de Saint Exupéry designed this work for grownups and graced it with images of friendship that we can each relate to. It's so short none of us can plead a *War and Peace* reason for not reading it. But to see life whole as the book intends, we have to get beyond the stuffy sophistication that would dismiss this tiny work as "kid stuff."

The children's book format is the ploy Saint Exupéry uses to wrench us away from our flow-charts and print-outs long enough to take life seriously. Children take life as it comes because they are completely open to the world annd refuse to funnel it to their own purposes with the Holland Tunnel vision of Wall Street entrepreneurs. They leave that to the bottom-liners of our time. Children know that the stream flowing from a jet plane is truly a white scar across the blue belly of heaven, as one first-grader described it until corrected by her teacher who got technical and called it contrail. Aesthetic vision is ever so much more valid than scientific analysis, which is bereft of beauty for being merely useful information. Airliners become the loveliest birds in the sky if a person can set aside his pragmatic outlook that would pare them down to aluminum alloy. Antoine de Saint Exupéry had already shown himself to be "a man's man" in his bravery over Arras for which he received the *Croix de Guerre*. What he required now of his mature readers was to shed their locked-in way of looking at things and to take on the grateful humility of a child who is aware of all the grandeur in God's creation and is puzzled by what adults seem to take so seriously, like stock indices, football tickets and certificates of deposit. If more husbands had listened to their wives as keenly as to financial reports, perhaps the U.S. divorce rate would not have kept pace with the high rolling of the 80s. A person with a head for figures can miss the beauty of the person who has been near all along; but he could never see *it* from his worldview of credit risks. Taking a chance on love is hard for someone whose outlook is hemmed in by bank balances. Antoine de Saint Exupéry tries to remind these hard-working good people that only friends count in the long run. He had rubbed elbows with such business commuters from

New York City because he too had had to change at Jamaica station to catch his train for Long Island. *Le Petit Prince* was meant for these Americans too. In fact, in another wartime irony, it appeared in English translation first.

The veteran pilot wrote his book in Northport, New York in the fall and early winter of 1942. Tongue in teeth, he drew the illustrations himself! There was a rose garden on the grounds—Antoine and his wife had moved there in September before frost claimed the last of the roses. Saint Exupéry could also see Long Island Sound from the den where he did his writing; its shoreline reminded him of his favorite retreat in the Libyan desert where he had crashed in 1936. A strand of sand has always provided the privacy where a person can listen with his heart for the values that prompt his living. There was only one for Antoine that could plumb the depths of one's uniqueness—the value of friendship. And there was only one way of finding it: through the appreciation perspective that frees a person for the self-donation that in full mutuality becomes the essence of friendship. His way of describing this way of knowing another in person has become his most widely quoted line: "A person can only see clearly with the heart—the essential is hidden from the eyes."[10] Saint Exupéry had distinguished this appreciation perspective from the functional attitude of the intellect in *Pilote de guerre*: "Only love can tell what image will come forth from the clay. Only love can direct a person towards that countenance. Intelligence has meaning only in implementing love."[11]

In *The Little Prince* the rose becomes his symbol for this beloved friend, as we discover in another line that captures the meaning of the non-utilitarian self-giving that forms friendship: "It is the time you have squandered upon your rose that makes your rose so special."[12] Being alone together with your beloved, strolling along a beach or through the woods or around a city block is completely useless because she is priceless—and in one such moment of profitless sharing she will know that you are not about exploiting her even for the satisfaction of her company or caress, and she will feel safe with you in a way she has not known perhaps ever before, and she can begin to trust you. Quietly, almost prayerfully sauntering along together, with maybe only an occasional glance towards one another and spontaneously placing a reassuring arm upon your beloved's shoulder, builds this trust that knows no timetable yet can never be rushed. This is the way she comes to know that she is the rose of your heart, unique in all this world—the rose Saint Exupéry first talks about in his classic of the Air-Age *Terre des hommes* (*Wind, Sand and Stars*): "When crossbreeding produces a new rose in a garden, all the gardeners are excited. They give the rose a special place where they nurture it."[13] As does the little prince whose devotion to his rose beamed through his whole being like candlelight, even when he was asleep.

Of course! The little prince confides to the aviator his secret of practical wisdom (which the French have ever imaged through the symbol of *renard*, the fox): "You are responsible forever for your rose."[14] The little prince's rose is at times more a thorn—a real pain—but she is no less precious to him for her poutiness or moods. Isn't it wonderful really to have a friend who trusts you enough when you phone not to put on a jovial air to mask her true feeling but just mopes along in speaking from her blue mood? Isn't it refreshing for you to know that she can count on you always being there for her, no matter how she feels and especially if she's in the pits? That's being responsible for your rose—responding to her as she is! Loving her as she is—for good. Because she is your rose.

Saint Exupéry images stars as flowers, so naturally the rose of his heart becomes his "star." The book speaks of stars—the guiding values in our lives. And about the person who is our star because he or she is always our friend. Antoine talks about the twinkling of this star as if it were a ringing bell resounding with the laughter of our friend. Poetic maybe, but isn't it true that the sparkle in your friend's eyes and the lilt of her gentle laughter fuse as your fond image of her as your "star?" I have a friend with whom I have spent many a Noël, whose spontaneous laugh, so delicate and warm and melodic, has the happy ring of a bell. The first I heard Saint Exupéry's meaning was from her—a decade after I had read his words. That's the beauty of his book; your friends new and old, keep supplying the meanings for his *wonder*ful phrases.

It is this refreshing laughter of your friend that keeps you from being dazzled by the other stars that streak across your heaven in the time of your living. Those other values beguile us with their appeal— the planets where the businessman, the geographer and king hold forth in their respective realms of money, organization and power. Up close these worlds turn cold because their terrain is desolate; no friendly voice is heard there. The logic of these domains pushes aside people who would be friends. The world of business sees the value of others only in their moneymaking prowess. The world of organization is where others are tapped only for their talent as contributing to the good of the company or team. Personal considerations are out of bounds—the rose as the image of the beloved is blotted from the game plan.

In this world of organization and competition, "winning is everything." This was the slogan of the late Green Bay Packer football coach, Vincent Lombardi, and unworthy of this good man. The maxim better fits the Caesars and is patently false because it would make all others losers and taint the meaning of victory. No—winning isn't everything because it creates its own cataracts and becomes blind to other considerations, sometimes even to the honest truth.

This mania for conquering all opposition has its hazards on the field of sport; it becomes horrendous when it extends to nations. Hitler, Himmler, and Goebbels all rejected the Catholic heritage into which they were baptized to make their nation the scourge of Europe. They were aware of their betrayal as they rolled over anyone who stood in their way, arresting men like Rupert Mayer and Konrad Adenauer early on and executing thousands like Albert Delp and Abbé Derry—as if to mask the horrors of the Holocaust.

France went down to defeat in 1940, as Saint Exupéry knew was inevitable, since 40 million farmers could not possibly withstand 80 million factory workers. But the Frenchmen did not turn their back on their heritage, as did the Nazis. They would suffer defeat and death to be the Calvary grain of wheat dying in the soil for a new Europe in the future—to invoke the image with which Saint Exupéry concludes *Pilote de guerre*: "Tomorrow, the onlooker would regard us as the vanquished. The vanquished have no claim to be heard. No more claim than the grain of wheat."[15]

How often in history have organizations been turned into power bases for the ambitious. The stunted logic of organization becomes the perfect tool for the king or dictator who treats all others as props for his thirst for power. This is the planet of the king whom Saint Exupéry exposes as having no identity unless he has people at hand to order around. The will to power is insatiable because there are always threats to it, which make it basically a defensive posture in spite of all its muscle-flexing. Nonconformity by any significant person or group becomes a problem for church or state because it would seem to threaten the position of those in authority. Even now we are dismayed at the exercise of power by certain Church officials who so quickly forget that Jesus was crushed by the religious power structure of his time because of his own nonconformity. In our own day, the ruins of the Berlin Wall bear bleak testimony to the fragile base upon which East German totalitarian power had rested. If Jesus came with the truth that would set us free, how often in history since his appearance has this freedom been abridged because of the will to power of churchmen and statesmen. Saint Exupéry lived and died in the pincers of such a worldwide power struggle; the king's planet was a shooting star that came to earth with a crash, leaving bomb craters pocking the terrain. Power always comes down as ash, even if it had been the most brilliant meteor in the sky.

Happily, our friend, like *l'etoile de berger*—the shepherd's star—is always present to us. But in searching for this star we must be wary of activities and gestures that masquerade as friendship. Like those of the lamplighter whom the little prince liked because he was interested in somebody besides himself and was willing to put out for others. But that glum man felt he had to earn friendship by helping the other in a round of services that became a race against time. For fear of ending up alone! His efforts, however, prove futile. A true friend cannot stand such attention because it glosses over her freckles as if she were a pedestal madonna and not her own everyday self standing on the same equal ground with the man she loves. Unlike the conceited man whom the little prince also encounters, she needs no vigil lights lit in her honor to reassure her of her own attractiveness. If a person does not have a sense of inner worth that allows her to believe herself lovable in the eyes of another, no amount of attention from that other will do. Without this faith in her interior beauty assuring her that she is belovable just as she is, she may resort to candlelight romance to image herself as "irresistible."

A good bit of our advertising clips and movie scenarios do suggest that a woman's or man's attentions can be won by setting up the appropriate sensual ambience with cocktails, late dinner, and cordials back at the apartment. Attentions for what? A night in bed together or even an affair? All this has little significance beyond fending off the loneliness each partner fears will be the outcome of the romance, because neither has the confidence that he or she could be loved for his or her own self. Not that sexual expression is not a genuine expression of total love in friendship. Saint Exupéry was marvelously free of the Manichaean taboos against sexuality that have afflicted Western culture since Augustine's time. So free, in fact, that it doesn't come up in his writings about friendship. He would agree with John Macmurray that "Sex-love, if it is love at all, is a personal communion in which a man and woman meet in the full integrity of their personal reality."[16] To engage in sexual expression before friendship is really formed is to use the partner for one's own self-gratification rather than to be loving towards her or him. To exploit another in this way, even if it is reciprocal, is to let desire pass as love. This is an elemental dishonesty to oneself and to the other and is the quickest way to short-circuit friendship.

To reduce others to objects for one's own sensual satisfaction is cause for the regrets some try to escape through drinking or drugs. Saint Exupéry depicts the remorse that self-gratification can foster by way of the character of the drunkard. (He deals only with this dimension of alcoholic abuse, without delving into the disease itself.) There is poignancy in his description of this lonely man who has despaired of forming loving associations. The guilt that afflicts him makes him feel an outcast—so much so that he can't even trust in the compassionate hand that would pull him out of the trough. The little prince does not linger long on the planet of the drunkard—perhaps because of the futility of associations built upon booze, drugs, and self-indulgence. No lasting world there because sensuality is episodic. No friendship either because the other is seen only as supplying gratification. No love because the world has narrowed back on self so exclusively that the capacity for gift has become flabby and sotted. Such a far and sad cry from the drink of friendship that Saint Exupéry looked forward to at war's end: "I need to elbow up next to you one more time on the banks of the Saône at the table of a small inn . . . where we will touch glasses in the peace of your smile as bright as the dawn."[17]

These lines are from the final pages Saint Exupéry saw published in his lifetime. He had written this *Lettre à un otage* to and for his friend Leon Woerth because, in the end, a person cannot talk about friendship without at some point being specific. Friendship is a value meant for all, but only a particular friend becomes one's personal star. For Antoine de Saint Exupéry, the symbol for this friend or any friend is his or her smile! Starsmile. If home is the welcoming shoulder of a friend, his or her smile is the sign of that welcome. Not even identical twins have the same smile because the smile springs from the heart of the person. A sincere smile is not calculated in the toothy way of TV anchormen and women. A smile is spontaneous and creates its own ambience of affection and friendship. Since Saint Exupéry's *Lettre à un otage* is a tribute to a special friend, it is almost natural to find at its core his hymn to a person's smile as the symbol of friendship:

A smile is often essential.
We are repaid with a smile.
We are rewarded with a smile.
We are inspired by a smile.
And the quality of a smile is such
that we would give our life for it.[18]

And Saint Exupéry did! For the smile of his farmer's niece, and Chris Gavoille with his huge grin on his baptismal day, and Leon Woerth's, and his mother's and that of his sister Didi, and, yes, even for that of his wife, though their relationship had gone into eclipse. And for the smiles of those other friends whose identities were too personal for public mention. They were all worth dying for and their smiles warmed his heart as he faded from the horizon that sunny day over the Côte d'Azur.

There was no logic to his being up in the sky that day. He was 14 years beyond the maximum age of 30 allowed for military pilots. But Saint Exupéry found that rule a bit illogical too—like so many things in war. For he had to do his part; he needed to let those he loved know that he was willing to risk his life for them to save their homes. In this he had for inspiration a young American pilot he had met in North Africa a year before. This 20-year-old flier had waited all through their supper together to bring up a question that had been bothering him. Then he hesitantly put it to Antoine: "If I accept the risk of being buried here, in my mind it's to give you back your country. Everyone has the right to live freely in his own country. And I am one with every person. But after my fellow Americans have helped give you back your house, will you help us in the Pacific?"[19]

Saint Exupéry put his arms around the young pilot who had that day completed his twenty-fifth mission after nearly being shot down. The veteran pilot never forgot the sincerity of this young American who was quite ready to give his life so that Saint Exupéry could go home—but who couldn't help thinking about his own countrymen trapped in the Pacific. Even as he repeated the incident to an American photojournalist, Saint Exupéry welled up. Such complete dedication from a 20-year-old. Saint Exupéry saw himself in the youth—20 and in Strasbourg learning to fly at the Polygon airfield. Getting fat on Alsatian food, as he wrote his mother, and taking on an Alsatian accent.[20] The young aviator had picked up the flagging spirits of the veteran, so much so that when Saint Exupéry finally got word that he could rejoin his old air group, he became exuberant with his hosts: "Don't you see, I'm young again . . . I'm 20 years old. Look how my hair has grown back in from the nape of my neck to the top of my head. It's because they've given me a young man's assignment. It's because I have the heart of a 20 year old."[21] There had been no logical reason for the American boy to be risking his life for France; except that in his uncomplicated vision he felt a bond with the people of France and with Saint Exupéry. So Antoine himself would go at it full tilt with all the energy and élan of his own heart of 20.

Saint Exupéry could have been writing of that young pilot when he remarks in *Pilote de guerre*, "Knowledge does not come of proof or explanation: It is to achieve a vision. But if we are to reach a vision, we must learn to participate in the search for that vision."[22] Not to cave into the logic that would save one's skin at all costs. No, quite the other way around, as Saint Exupéry found out in that mission over Arras: "If I had turned around a moment earlier, I would never have come to know myself. I would never have experienced the tender affection that now fills my heart. I am flying back to persons I belong to. I am going home."[23]

Antoine had realized that if we sacrifice for no one, we belong to no one: "If I insist upon serving only myself, I will not be forming a bond with anyone and, consequently, I shall be nothing."[24] Not that your friend requires your gift—friendship can never be a duty—but you need to become one with him or her and this comes only in the experience of risking all for that special person. There is no other way—which is why prenuptial property arrangements can cast a self-oriented shadow over a marital union at the outset. Saint Exupéry's ordeal over Arras brought him back to basics: "We have to give before we can receive . . . I enkindled my love for my people through the gift of my blood during that sortie . . . This is the mystery, that to instill love we must begin with sacrifice."[25] But not sacrifice in the ascetic sense, which is much too self-conscious. No, sacrifice in the sense of cherishing your beloved as the love of your life to whom you spontaneously make total gift.[26]

Individualistic logic cannot fathom this. So those who yield to such self-serving considerations will never know the joy and peace and sense of fulfillment experienced in the union created in the mutuality of total self-giving. The consummate egotist will never know another as true friend because he will never have known himself as a giving friend nor will be even aware of the sacrifice she has already made for him. Nor will he even know God, for all his protestation that he has done all his duties before God and humankind. Saint Exupéry was wise enough to realize that since God is love we only experience him in the ties of human relationship formed in total mutual gift. We could never know that we were the beloved of God if we had never been touched with the affection of a person whose spontaneous concern was reassurance that God's spirit of love was still vibrant in our antiseptic world. Love and sacrifice know no logic. Nor does the mutual self-donation that forms the bond of friendship.

This spirit of love that springs from the core of a man, woman or child is in a sense the only reality in our personal world. For just as the smile is the symbol of that person's uniqueness, his or her spirit of love is the expression of that uniqueness that is his or hers only. Whatever would suppress this would make our world barren and without significance and untouched with the divinity that is the spirit of divine love. Creeds don't count if affection dries up. We'll never find God in creeds if the spirit of love is constrained, even in the name of such creeds. Antoine confronted that ultimate temptation and called it by its name: "Personal fulfillment has to do with the Spirit, not the intellect. The spirit knows how to love but it is asleep . . . Temptation is the urge to yield to intellectual reasons when the spirit is asleep."[27]

So every time Saint Exupéry crunched his bone-weary frame into the cockpit of his reconnaissance plane, he was being true to his spirit and making his way home. In the only way he knew—by putting his life on the line for his beloved so they could be at home when he finally got there. Every flight for him was meant for this return, as he remarks of the Breton sailors in his *Lettre à un otage*: "It was their return they were preparing as they hoisted the sails for their outward-bound voyage."[28] The beacon before the eyes of those sailors was the light in the window of the fiancée that kept shining beyond Cape Horn to the Pacific until they should lay anchor again in the harbor at Brest. The star before Saint Exupéry's pensive eyes as Lieutenant Leleu helped him into the P-38 for those final missions was that cluster of friends close to his heart—those to whom he had yearned to say "I love you" in person. For Saint Exupéry it was always the star of the little prince, the star of Christmas, the star of belonging: "We are hurrying back to a little celebration. A light burning in a far-off cottage window changes the harshest winter night into Christmas Eve."[29]

If you are away for a long while from those who mean most, you can relate to those airborn (sic!) lines of the poetic pilot. I do—for having been away a long year in Strasbourg, even over Christmastide. But I would be flying soon to a pilot's home where his wife and child would greet me and to a reunion with those other persons who fill out the star in my heart. I would be leaving behind those fond others in Strasbourg who could well be the children or grandchildren of Saint Exupéry's friends from the 20s. The family downstairs with whom I spent Christmas Eve and my student friends at the University who fully accepted me as an auditor in their French literature class. The petite Lycéenne next door who shyly showed me her "A" paper in English and who has since become an "A-plus" person in my life. My *cordonnier* (shoemaker) Georges who drove me to the wayside monument to the American soldiers who gave their last and best for France.

And Julie. We rode the same bus often and from the first she welcomed me with her gentle glance as if I really belonged in Alsace and on that bus. Not that we ever spoke over the months. But a few weeks before I left Strasbourg, we had a chance to talk for a moment at the bus-stop on Place Broglie. And she entrusted me with her name. She couldn't have been more than 12 and said she was to have a class in "*couture*" that afternoon. Symbolic because in her simple acceptance of an American with halting French, she had woven a tie with me that keeps to this day. It was a shining moment in springtime, the kind Saint Exupéry meant in saying: "I have simply come to rest for five minutes of eternity in friendship."[30] Her name's day is May 22nd—the anniversary of Saint Exupery's flight over Arras. Julie could have been the farmer's niece for whom Antoine was ready to give his life that day. Her grandmother may have had her first chocolate bar from an American soldier that Christmas of 1944 before he and seven thousand G.I.'s like him would die to save Alsace. That soldier would have agreed with Saint Exupéry that the gracious smile of Julie was worth dying for. Just as Jesus willingly went to his death under the tender gaze of his mother—O *dulcis, o clemens, o pie Maria,* as they still sing in the cathedral of Notre Dame de Strasbourg.

Saint Exupéry's mother's name was Marie too. His closing words to her in that last letter were "Kiss me, Maman, as I do you from the bottom of my heart."[31] Home for Antoine Marie-Roger de Saint Exupéry was his mother's welcoming shoulder where he first knew belonging. And where he was heading when his life came full circle—flying home!

Endnotes

Chapter 1: Home

1. Antoine de Saint Exupéry, *Lettre à un otage* (Paris Gallimard, 1945), 25. Translation by Philip Mooney.

2. Ibid.

3. Antoine de Saint Exupéry, *Pilote de guerre* (Paris: Gallimard, 1942), 236. Translation by Phillp Mooney.

4. Tennessee Williams, *The Niqht of the Iguana* (New York: New Directions, 1962), 108-109.

5. Saint Exupéry, *Lettre à un otage*, 68.

6. cf. Phillip Shaver and Carin Rubenstein, *In Search of Intimacy* (New York: Delacorte, 1982).

7. Brendan, Behan, *The Borstal Boy* (New York: Random House, 1971), Adapted for the stage by Frank McMahon, 118.

Chapter 2: Institutions

1. John Macmurray, *Reason and Emotion* (London: Faber and Faber, 1935), 96.

2. "Pastoral Constitution on the Church in the Modern World": Part I: The Church and Man s Calling; Chapter IV: The Role of the Church in the Modern World: #43; *The Documents of Vatican II*, Walter M. Abbott, S.J., ed., Joseph Gallagher, dir. tr. (New York: America Press, 1966), 244.

3. Macmurray, *Reason and Emotion*, 138.

4. John Macmurray, *The Clue to History* (London: Harper, 1939), 163-164.

5. Ibid., 158.

6. Macmurray, *Reason and Emotion*, 65.

Chapter 3: Knowing You— Knowing Me

1. Anne Morrow Lindbergh, *Gift from the Sea* (New York: Pantheon, 1955).

2. Antoine de Saint Exupéry, *Terre des hommes* (Paris: Gallimard, 1939), 217. Translation by Philip Mooney.

3. Antoine de Saint Exupéry, *Le Petit Prince* (Paris: Gallimard, 1959), 474. Translation by Philip Mooney.

4. John Macmurray, *The Self as Agent* (London: Faber and Faber, 1957), 15.

5. Saint Exupéry, *Pilote de guerre*, 168.

6. Macmurray, *Reason and Emotion*, 8.

7. Harry Guntrip, *Psychology for Ministers and Social Workers* (London: Independent Press, 1949), 164.

8. Williams, *The Niqht of the Iguana*, 49.

9. Macmurray, *Reason and Emotion*, 31.

10. Saint Exupéry, *Pilote de guerre*, 197-198; 203-205.

11. Philip Roth, *Goodbye Columbus* (New York: Bantam, 1959), 97.

12. Guntrip, *Psychology for Ministers*, 161-162.

13. Macmurray, *Reason and Emotion*, 137-138.

14. Saint Exupéry, *Terres des hommes*, 202-203.

Chapter 4: Three Attitudes

1. Myles Connolly, "Lines for a Guestbook," *America,* (April 25, 1936), 61.

2. Macmurray, *Reason and Emotion*, 151.

3. N. Richard Nash, *The Rainmaker* (New York: Random House, 1955), 101.

4. Saint Exupéry, *Le Petit Prince*, 474.

5. Ibid.

6. Thomas Butler Feeney, "Favorites," *When the Wind Blows* (New York: Dodd, Mead, 1947), 3.

7. Miguel de Unamuno, *The Agony of Christianity and Essays on Faith: Selected Works of Miguel de Unamuno*, Vol. 5, Anthony Kerrigan tr. (London: Routledge and Kegan Paul, 1974), 56.

8. Ibid., 58.

9. Saint Exupéry, *Lettre à un otage*, 31.

10. Jean Radcliffe, *Will There Ever be a Morning* (New York: Prentice Hall, 1965), 156.

11. Nash, *The Rainmaker*, 56.

Chapter 5: Distancing and Appreciation

1. Feeney, "Vision," *When the Wind Blows*, 29.

2. Tad Mosel, *All the Way Home* (New York: Samuel French, 1961), 13.

3. Ibid., 31.

4. William Butler Yeats, "The Lover Tells of the Rose in His Heart," *The Collected Poems of W.B. Yeats* (New York: Macmillan, 1956), 5

5. Saint Exupéry, *Lettre à un otage*, 19.

6. Ian Suttie, *The Origins of Love and Hate* (New York: Julian Press, 1935), 85.

7. Mosel, *All the Way Home,* 55.

8. Ibid., 68.

9. Ibid., 72.

10. Karl Rahner, S.J., *Theological Investigations IV*, Kevin Smyth, tr. (London: Darton, Longman and Todd, 1966), 119-120.

11. Saint Exupéry, *Petit Prince*, 474.

12. John Macmurray, *Persons in Relation* (London: Faber and Faber, 1961), 29.

Chapter 6: Duty and Affection

1. Terrence Rattigan, *In Praise of Love* (New York: Samuel French, 1973), 78.
2. Guntrip, *Psychology for Ministers*, 162.
3. Rattigan, *In Praise of Love*, 73.
4. Ibid.
5. Rattigan, *In Praise of Love*, 81.
6. Antoine de Saint Exupéry, *Citadelle* (Paris: Gallimard, 1948), 24. Translation by Philip Mooney.
7. Rattigan, *In Praise of Love*, 81
8. Suttie, *The Origins of Love and Hate*, 89-90.

Chapter 7: Searching Significance

1. Sara Bradford, *Princess Grace* (New York: Stein and Day, 1984), 218.
2. Herbert Marcuse, *Eros and Civilization* (New York: Random House, 1961), 88.
3. John Macmurray, *Search for Reality in Religion* (London: Friends Home Service Committee, 1965), 77.
4. Antoine de Saint Exupéry, *Carnets* (Paris: Gallimard, 1975), 29. Translation by Philip Mooney.
5. Karl Rahner, S.J., *The Christian in the Marketplace*, Cecily Hastings, tr. (New York: Sheed and Ward, 1963), 24.

Chapter 8: What Is Failure Anyway?

1. Saint Exupéry, *Pilote de guerre*, 240.
2. Ibid., 52.
3. Mary Cunningham, *Powerplay* (New York: Simon and Schuster, 1984), 277.
4. Frank Gilroy, *The Subject Was Roses* (New York: Random House, 1965), 200.
5. Ibid., 201.
6. Ibid., 200.
7. John Macmurray, *Creative Society* (New York: Association Press, 1936), 99.
8. Cunningham, *Powerplay*, 284-285.
9. Brigitte Bardot, "Le Mythe B.B." *Studio* No. 11 (February 1988), 43. Translation by Philip Mooney.
10. Saint Exupéry, *Carnets*, 157.
11. Alfred Delp, S.J., *The Prison Meditations of Father Albert Delp*, intro. by Thomas Merton (New York: Herder, 1963), 173.

Chapter 9: The Down and Out Corner of Kindness

1. Macmurray, *Persons in Relation*, 63
2. Emile Zola, *L 'Assommoir* (Paris: Garnier-Flammarion,1969), 70.

3. Malcolm Lowry, *Under the Volcano* (New York: Plume, 1971), 218.

4. Williams, *Night of the Iguana*, 81.

5. Guntrip, *Psychology for Ministers*, 161.

6. Wiiliams, *Night of the Iguana*, 110-111.

7. Ibid., 81.

8. Ibid., 97.

9. Ibid., 104.

10. Saint Exupéry, *Lettre à un otage*, 59-60.

11. Williams, *Night of the Iguana*, 115-116.

12. Ibid., 127.

13. Peter Coutros, "An Obit for a Decent Man," *The New York Daily News,* (January 17, 1973).

Chapter 10: Leaving Home

1. Thomas A. Daly, "The Song of the Thrush," *Canzoni.* (Philadelphia: David McKay, 1914), 26.

2. Elizabeth Goudge, *Gentian Hill* (New York: Coward McCann, 1949), 70.

3. Macmurray, *Reason and Emotion*, 131.

4. Brian Friel, Philadelphia, *Here I Come* (New York: Farrar, Straus and Giroux, 196

5. Ibid., 32.

6. Ibid., 38.

7. Friel, *Philadelphia*, 85.

8. Ibid., 113.

Chapter 11: Beginning Again

1. Saint Exupéry, *Pilote de guerre*, 189-190.

2. Saint Exupéry, *Lettre à un otage* , xx.

3. William Butler Yeats, *Plays and Controversies* (New York: Macmillan, 1924), 131.

4. John Bannister Tabb, "An Idolator," *The Best Poems of John Bannister Tabb* (Westminster, Maryland: Newman, 1954), 122.

5. Gibson Winter, *Love and Conflict* (New York: Doubleday, 1958), 111-112.

6. Macmurray, *Reason and Emotion*, 101.

7. Jules Toner, S.J., *The Experience of Love* (Washington: Corpus, 1968), 127.

8. Macmurray, *Reason and Emotion*, 159.

9. Robert Johann, *The Meaning of Love* (Glen Rock, NJ: Paulist Press, 1966), 19.

10. Sydney Harris, "We Don't See What is There" *The Detroit Free Press,* (January 4, 1966).

11. Macmurray, *Reason and Emotion*, 47

12. Saint Exupéry, *Terre des hommes*, 202-203.

Chapter 12: Flying Home

1. Antoine de Saint Exupéry, *Ecritures de guerre*, (Paris: Gallimard, 1982), 516. Translation by Philip Mooney.

2. Ibid. 516-17.

3. Saint Exupéry, *Pilote de guerre*, 168.

4. Saint Exupéry, *Ecritures de guerre*, 515.

5. Marie-Madeleine Mast, "Le Baptême de Christian," *Icare* (No. 96: 1981), 140. Translation by Philip Mooney.

6. Saint Exupéry, *Ecritures de guerre*, 512.

7. Saint Exupéry, *Pilote de guerre*, 240.

8. Ibid., 202.

9. Saint Exupéry, *Petit Prince*, 489.

10. Ibid., 474.

11. Saint Exupéry, *Pilote de guerre*, 205.

12. Saint Exupéry, *Petit Prince*, 474.

13. Saint Exupéry, *Terre des hommes*, 217.

14. Saint Exupéry, *Petit Prince*, 476.

15. Saint Exupéry, *Pilote de guerre*, 246.

16. Macmurray, *Reason and Emotion*, 141.

17. Saint Exupéry, *Lettre à un otage*, 69.

18. Ibid., 41.

19. Antoine de Saint Exupéry, "Lettre à un Americain," *Icare* (No. 96: 1981), 133. Translation by Philip Mooney.

20. Antoine de Saint Exupéry, *Lettres à sa mère* (Paris: Gallimard, 1957), 116. Translation by Philip Mooney.

21. Saint Exupéry, *Ecritures de guerre*, 493.

22. Saint Exupéry, *Pilote de guerre*, 54.

23. Ibid., 179.

24. Ibid., 235.

25. Ibid., 240.

26. Ibid., 231.

27. Ibid., 52.

28. Saint Exupéry, *Lettre à un otage*, 19.

29. Saint Exupéry, *Pilote de guerre*, 196.

30. Saint Exupéry, *Ecritures de guerre*, 503.

31. Ibid., 512.